Studies on the Development of Consciousness

Studies on the Development of Consciousness

Yves Chesni, M.D.

Specialist in Nervous and Mental Diseases
Former director of the Service Médico-Pédagogique, Geneva, Switzerland
Vice-President of the International Stress Management Association
Member of the New York Academy of Sciences

Translated from the French by
Joseph P. Zenk, Ph.D.

THE LIVE OAK PRESS, PALO ALTO

Published by The Live Oak Press,
Postal Box 60036, Palo Alto, California U.S.A. 94306

Library of Congress Cataloging-in-Publication Data
Chesni, Yves.
   [Recherches sur le développement de la conscience. English]
   Studies on the development of consciousness / Yves Chesni ;
translated from the French by Joseph P. Zenk.
        p.   cm.
   Translation of: Recherches sur le développement de la conscience.
   Includes bibliographical references.
   ISBN 0-931095-02-6 : $37.50 (est.)
   1. Consciousness.   2. Psychoanalysis.   I. Title.
  BF311.C51713 1992
  150--dc20   91-32903
                                              CIP

MANUFACTURED IN THE UNITED STATES OF AMERICA

Also by Yves Chesni:

Dialectical Realism: Towards a Philosophy of Growth, translated by Joseph P. Zenk. The Live Oak Press, Palo Alto, 1987.(ISBN 0-931095-00-X, Library of Congress card number 86-277726)

The Neurological Examination of the Infant, in cooperation with André-Thomas and S. Saint-Anne Dargassies, translated and edited by R. C. MacKleith, P. E. Polani, and E. Clayton-Jones. The Spastic Society and Heinemann, London, 1960, reprinted 1964.

Travaux du Service Médico-Pédagogique de Genève, in cooperation with F. Naville, M. Fert, C. Balavoine, A. Menthonnex, R. Guyot, S. Dupuis, E. Amblet, A. Paunier, F. Guignard, F. Martin, A. Grillet. Reprinted from *Médecine et Hygiène,* Médecine et Hygiène, Geneva, 1957.

Réalisme dialectique. Introduction à une philosophie de la croissance. La Baconnière, Neuchâtel, 1973. (Library of Congress card number 74-159365.)

Recherches sur le développement de la conscience. La Baconnière, Neuchâtel, 1983. (ISBN 2-8252-0208-8, Library of Congress card number 85-101900.) Translated here.

In memory of Dr. Daniel Douady, former Director of the Fondation Santé des Etudiants de France, who managed to give me some time.

In memory of Dr. Edmund Jacobson, former Director of the Chicago Laboratory for Clinical Physiology, who helped me in its use.

Contents

Preface to the American Edition, ix

Preface, xi

PART ONE—REFLECTIONS CONCERNING CONSCIOUSNESS, 1

Chapter I. Consciousness and Reflection on Consciousness, 4

Chapter II. Differentiation-Correlation-Consciousness, 22

PART TWO—PSYCHOANALYSIS AND FREEDOM, 41

Chapter III. Innate and Learned Automatisms.
Growth in Consciousness and Freedom, 44

Chapter IV. Neurotic Obstacles to the Growth of Consciousness
and Liberty, 58

Chapter V. Summary, 74

PART THREE—A TENTATIVE INTERPRETATION OF ST. JOHN
OF THE CROSS WITHIN NATURAL, OPEN PERSPECTIVES, 77

Chapter VI. Biological Background, 79

Chapter VII. Spiritual Background, 84

Chapter VIII. St. John of the Cross, 92

Chapter IX. Conclusions, 113

PART FOUR—The GOALS, METHODS, AND
LIMITS OF PSYCHOTHERAPY, 117

Chapter X. Neurotic Automatisms, 119

Chapter XI. Technics and Effects of Analytical Psychotherapy,
Progressive Relaxation, Systematic Desensitization, and Synthetic
Approaches, 124

Chapter XII. Philosophical Points of View, 131

PART FIVE—CONSCIOUSNESS AND MOVEMENT: STUDIES
CONCERNING THE MOTOR COMPONENT OF INNER SPEECH
AND VISUAL IMAGINATION, 139

Preface to the American Edition

In the five conferences here reproduced, the author has treated some selected points in the development of consciousness, with special emphasis on the perspectives of critical philosophy, psychology, psychotherapy, and spirituality.

The first conference situates the study of consciousness. Contrary to Descartes and Husserl, the realist philosopher does not cast doubt on the existence of the world, other people, his own body, and a large part of his own consciousness. Contrary to Kant, he does not believe that he is separated from things by his own sensorial and intellectual structures. Like Aristotle, he sees in knowledge the common act of a subject capable of knowing and an object capable of being known, but for all that he does not despair of his ability to determine the respective parts played by each of the two factors. Contrary to physiological reductionism, he does not pretend to understand a system that is endowed with consciousness and yet abstracts from consciousness. Contrary to the absurdity of solipsism, he infers a consciousness more or less analogous to his own among his peers and a number of other animal species. In consciousness he perceives simultaneously a sign, a consequence, and a factor of differentiation and correlation, a higher form of unity requiring, respecting, and promoting the originality of the parts.

The second and fourth conferences deal with the fetters of neuroses in human development and their suppression, through psychoanalysis—

which is a part of "cognitive therapy"—behavioral psychotherapy, or through the one and the other conjointly. These neurotic automatisms, repetitive, unconscious, involuntary and coercive—the contrary of free behavior—result from the unfortunate conjunction of an inadequate environment during infancy and from certain hereditary virtualities, particularly the tendency to react totally to signs isolated from context, as new-born children and instinctual animals do, who still have only minimal intelligence and are adapted by means of innate behaviors served up whole and entire by the evolution of species. While shedding light on their prevention or treatment, the understanding of neurotic mechanisms contributes at the same time to that of normal development: i.e., the growth within us of the power to grasp the whole, to situate the parts in their relationships with each other and in respect to the whole, to be neither blinded nor bound by any of them; the power within us, to put it succinctly, of expanding that inner freedom that penetrates, humanizes, and enlarges our humblest joys.

The third conference speaks of spirituality. In every age throughout the entire world, spiritual men and women have desired to wipe out the obstacles, and not only the neurotic ones, to inner freedom: "If you stop at something," St. John of the Cross counsels us, "you fail to push forward towards the All." It is the purgative way that attempts to rid us of all pettiness in order that we might be attuned to the essential, to the All, that we may even, as Christian mystics believe, be rendered "divine by participation." But opinions differ regarding the nature of the All, the place of man within and in respect to the All, and the possibility of knowing the All—which is not the same as knowing all.

Thought has a neuro-motor aspect. It disappears, completely or selectively, as the eye and speech muscles relax. This "relaxation of the mind," this putting to rest of the spirit, is, according to Jacobson, the essential element of progressive relaxation. It is not foreign to the technics of spiritual disencumberment, purification, and perfecting at issue in the following chapters. Such is the object of the fifth conference.

The author expresses the hope that this modest effort will be of some usefulness.

Preface

Our highest activity is linked to consciousness and disappears with it. In this latter case, however, a number of vital activities persist, and physiology teaches us that, even when we are awake, a large part of our normal functioning remains unconscious. It is about the unconscious nature of a number of our deepest motives, whether healthy or pathological, normal or neurotic, that psychoanalysis, Pavlovian reflexology, and ethology, the science of comparative behavior, speak to us. Along with them genetic epistemology helps us to understand the psychological growth of children and animals; botany, for its part, dares not infer a consciousness analogous to ours among plants, no matter how close they are to us in certain respects. Sociology views the world in terms of the growth of civilization's goods, the Third World of Popper, unconscious in itself but the result of consciousness and a possible source of consciousness, spiritual enrichment and true happiness, as well as one of emptiness, illusion, and injustice. Our engineers provide us with computers, sophisticated and unconscious extensions of ourselves. Nothing stops us from imagining that some day these may be programmed to reproduce and perfect themselves without us, and that man will little by little become a simple appendage, vaguely conscious, of some machine of yore invented by a race long since vanished, by men who here and there had tried to manipulate the multitude... In fact, History foreshadows an entirely different evolution, allowing us to anticipate an entirely different future, and to hope for it.

A supplement of information and motivation, an interiorization of actions that allows reversible operations...: perhaps it makes some sense to ask what is the purpose of consciousness. But let us not forget that even though it does make for a quantitative increase in performances according to other criteria, what consciousness brings to living beings above all is itself: a qualitative change.

At Annecy, Chicago, and Geneva, between 1975 and 1979, I gave five conferences on some selected points about the development of consciousness from a multidisciplinary perspective. Four of them were published in professional reviews and are here produced with the kind permission of Mr. Emile Callot, President of the Cercle d'Etudes Philosophiques d'Annecy, and Professor F. G. McGuigan, Director of the Performance Research Laboratory of the University of Louisville and Executive Director of the American Association for the Advancement of Tension Control*. The fifth, given before the Groupe Genevois de la Société Romande de Philosophie, appears in print for the first time.

Saint Philbert de Grand Lieu, May 8, 1980.

---

* Presently Director of the Institute for Stress Management, International United States University, San Diego, California.

PART ONE

Reflections Concerning Consciousness*

*Conference given March 23, 1977, at the
Cercle d'Etudes Philosophiques d'Annecy
(Conférences et Débats, 2, 1977).

Among the pitfalls to be avoided in the study of consciousness special attention should be given to phenomenology, apriorism, confusionism, and physiological reductionism. In the foreground is the pitfall of solipsism, the absurd idea that I could be the sole existent or the only one endowed with consciousness.

Through the *transcendental phenomenological reduction* the phenomenologist, for various reasons, "puts in parentheses" the world, his body, and everything within his consciousness that lacks "apodictic, adequate, perfect, certain, and present evidence." He thus reduces his horizon of certainty to the thin slice of the "now" of a fixation amnesia, excluding from the outset of his investigation the possibility of a supreme principle of explanation: i.e., the real relation between real existents, a relation whose phenomenological "intention" is but a doubtful, isolated, and wavering fragment. Others do not doubt the existence of an "exterior" reality yet believe themselves enclosed under the double seal of the *a priori forms and categories* of their sensibility and their intelligence (a contradiction in the opinion of Husserl). By an astounding pleonasm, consciousness would be able to know nothing but itself. Others such as Aristotle clearly see in consciousness the "common act" shared by an existent able to know and one able to be known. But they lapse into *confusionism,* despairing of any ability to distinguish the respective roles of each of them, and consequently risk *de facto* falling into the positions described above. *Physiological reductionism,* for its part, purports to understand a system capable of conscious relations without considering them. "It thinks," said Freud, "that it can establish a psychology that does not take that fundamental fact into account." By neglecting a characteristic of the system which it studies, it errs in respect to levels.

Solipsism is avoided without any "problem" and without any "demonstration" simply by refusing to step foot within it, and mental solipsism by *inference.* The latter deduces, with greater or lesser necessity, from the likeness or analogy of other aspects, structures, or performances, a likeness or analogy of consciousness. As is the case in all science (including even that of our own consciousness), inference is not coincidence. Like that of the various sciences, its degree of certitude varies.

Once these obstacles have been overcome and we have been warned, consciousness can be recognized for what it is: a characteristic of original related psychophysiological systems, in a certain way growing, connoting the evolution of species, individuals, societies and civilizations. In a word, it is a characteristic that connotes History from a certain degree of development, throughout convergent, divergent, or contrary movements. This is what the law of *differentiation-correlation-consciousness* seeks to express, where consciousness appears at once as a sign, a consequence, and an agent of differentiation and correlation, as a higher form of unity implying, respecting, and promoting the originality of the parts.

CHAPTER I

Consciousness and Reflection on Consciousness

Reflective consciousness and non-reflective consciousness.

For many of us consciousness, the highest level of consciousness, is what characterizes man. Without consciousness man is nothing but a dormant body, comatose or dead, a tool in an assembly line, a gear in a machine, a remote-controlled robot, a few random molecules dispersed in the great All.

This does not mean that man, whether he believes in his eternal destiny or not, may or even ought not sacrifice all or a part of his consciousness to the point of giving up his very life for some causes that surpass him. This does not mean that civilization, even though it is created by men and, in principle, for men, does not in a certain fashion transcend the consciousness of each and of all. Neither does it mean that our consciousness bears no risk of dispersion, illusion, error, or illness, or that it may not connote remoteness or separation, and a sort of weakening or diminution of being. Still less does it mean in a cry of arrogance, despair, or the will to "absolute knowledge," that my consciousness alone is certain, or a small fragment of it, that everything else, the world, my body, and even a major part of my consciousness might be nothing more than a dream, a solitary and fleeting delirium, and that there may exist nothing other than what appears to me.

Consciousness, or interior, mental life, is *sui generis,* i.e., undefinable. It is fundamentally relational and the various kinds of relations serve to nuance it qualitatively: sensation, gnosia or non-verbal recognition, denomination, visual and verbal thought, remembrance, imagination, fantasy, mental operations, reasoning, hunger, thirst, desire, fear, anger, hate, love, interest, appeasement, satisfaction, aesthetic emotion, etc. You know as well as I do what these words embrace, by *experience*. I do not wish to say that our interior lives are identical; I am at least certain that they are analogous or I would not have agreed to give this lecture or have written these lines. I will shortly pursue at greater length the matter of *inferring* the consciousness of others.

All consciousness is "consciousness of something" (the phenomenologists say intentional, we say relational) and is at the same time "consciousness of itself," i.e., coincidence with itself,[1] and here we are in agreement with the phenomenological description. As I observed in a work written in a different context,[2] *non-reflective* and *reflective* consciousness differ by one degree of reflection. This excluding of coincidence (as well as separation) is the lot of all knowledge, and of any other relationship as well. The same applies to the relationship of self to self, to the knowledge of one's own consciousness and *a fortiori* of consciousness of the other.

Nevertheless, according as one either can or cannot "do two different things at the same time," a distinction thrusts itself upon us, one valid for other forms of knowing as well. It is possible to speak, write, describe, draw, and paint while at the same time considering, seeing, and imagining visually; it is not possible to speak either aloud or interiorly two different sentences at one and the same time. To these possibilities or impossibilities of psychological simultaneity there correspond correlative possibilities or impossibilities on the part of the body for different simultaneous physiological activities within defined anatomical systems, or for one system acting as a substitute for another.[3] Thus, depending on the case, and this includes instances of self-observation, certain modalities of consciousness are or are not exclusive of each other. It seems to me that Sartre's technic of auto-observation applies more to the first case. This consists in "resuscitating" some states of consciousness, in trying to revive them while observing them "out of the corner of one's eye."[1] I cannot examine this distinction with any greater detail at this time. I merely add that in all cases the reflective consciousness no longer coincides with the non-reflective consciousness, which is the object of its study, and yet is not separated from it. As for whether the one modifies the other, this is a question I will take up later when considering confusionism.

It has been said that reflection marks the passage from "naïve" realism to "critical" philosophy, and that in a way modern philosophy begins with the Greek and Roman sceptics.[4] It is true that this was an important moment in the history of thought. But we think that at this point we were offered two options, one of which, aberrant in our opinion, has flirted with solipsism or has quickly led to it. Prior to that moment or succeeding it, whether taking it into account or not, there are also, perhaps as old as man himself, the wisdom, technics, and practices of spiritual, interior men of all times and places. And there are also the moral sciences, the methods of spiritual examination and direction, of training, rehabilitating, and curing consciences, right up to modern psychology, psychoanalysis, and psychiatry. As for Eccles,[5] he joins several others in relating man's first efforts at self-reflection with the first evidence of burials during the Early Paleolithic Period two hundred thousand to a million years ago, when our Neanderthal ancestor was working with flint, living in caves and burying his dead in them... Teilhard de Chardin, in his usual lofty perspective, equates the dawn of humanity with self-reflection.[6] Catholic children make their confessions and partake in communion from the age of seven, but brief examinations of conscience, along with night prayers, often begin earlier. But should we not go still further? Is there not a kind of seminal awareness of the consciousness of the other in that generalized intersubjectivity that we have been led to infer among animals, at least among the highest of them?

Some distortions of reflection on consciousness.

The immense progress represented by the reflective step has not come about without some negative impact. Like all knowledge, knowledge about consciousness can be used "for good or for evil," for the liberation or the enslavement of men's consciousness, and we still have sad examples of its misuse staring us in the face. Brute force, as well as the most subtle psychological methods of influence, have been placed at the service of falsehood, and they continue to be. "Das Alleräusserste ist, dass man ihm die Instrumente zeigt," said the pope apropos of making Galileo abjure the truth, and the Inquisitor responded "Das wird genügen, Eure Heiligkeit. Herr Galilei versteht sich auf Instrumente."[7] We are not far from Stalin's trials.

Today I want to focus on another aspect of the question, viz., that kind of narcissistic fascination that their own consciousness exerts on certain thinkers. Lorenz explains this overly radical introversion as follows: when he achieved the ability to reflect upon himself, man became so interested in this new "object" that he has sometimes had the tendency to forget...all the rest.[8] Reality is perhaps not all that simple.

The transcendental phenomenological reduction.
Some motives behind it.

> *Some of my cousins who had the great advantage of University education,* Churchill writes, *used to tease me with arguments to prove that nothing has any existence except what we think of it...* K. Popper.[9]

Actually, the phenomenologist does not deny the existence of the world, his body, and everything that his consciousness does not reveal as an "apodictic, adequate, perfect, certain, and present evidence."[10] Quite simply, he pretends to have the ability to doubt it. In order not to build his philosophical abode upon the sand, he abstains, he makes no judgment of existence, he "places existence between parentheses"and acts as if it did not exist. Let us note in passing that this is equivalent to a practical negation and has led some to one that is theoretical as well. Whether they doubt or deny existence, the phenomenologists thus align themselves against the affirmation of all other instances of consciousness, calling this affirmation "naïve" and anti-philosophical. What can be the motives for such an extraordinary attitude?

In my opinion the motives for the "existential doubt" are of three kinds: Fashion, illness, and the desire for perfection. I do not mean to say that people interested in *fashion* and patients suffering from existential doubt are phenomenologists, nor that the latter are interested in *fashion* or ill. Among my friends and masters I count philosophers who are genuine phenomenologists;[11] I know that they will approve of my using this occasion to treat the question of existential doubt in all its breadth, and, to begin with, that doubt as it exists within persons who are not philosophers.

I will touch upon *fashion* only briefly. As for those who repeat without understanding, for whom it is the style to use the language of phenomenology, I agree with Sartre. They do not pursue the reduction "seriously." I will add that a number of them are quite ignorant about it, claiming to be phenomenologists yet at the same time misunderstanding phenomenology in its very essence. For me this category does not include those who honestly attempt to reconcile contrary positions by constructing, for example, a "realist phenomenology" or a "phenomenological realism"; but I cannot prevent myself from thinking that they are unknowingly guilty of a contradiction, speaking of square circles or rectangular triangles.*[12] The matter of *illness* (I am a physician) will occupy me at somewhat greater length.

Hell, Christians tell us, is the absence of love, of charity, i.e., confinement within oneself. Hell, says Sartre, is other people, and that brings up some of the most remarkable examples of neurotic mechanisms: dissociation, projection, and particularly "the unconscious outward deflection of the death wish"—defensive escape, denial, or the conviction of omnipotence.[13] One of my young patients, who was in the grip of an intense oral aggressiveness, used to defend himself by isolating his evil side and projecting it outwards. The world had become his persecutor, filled with ogres and devouring beasts, and as a defense against it he imagined himself all-powerful, a great magician, God, and even "more than God." He used this omnipotence in the most rational way, reducing his enemies to the size of a mouse or making them *disappear*. However, when he had inadvertently suppressed not just monstrous parental images but his actual parents, he then set about to revive them. To put it another way, his good side, the loving part of him, recreated, indeed, *created* the world. As Lorenz and Popper put it[8, 9] speaking of those who deny existence, those creators of "the universe within themselves," "for themselves," this poor child appeared as a megalomaniac and a blasphemer.

In a less radically reductionist way, one of my patients limited herself to physical *isolation,* never leaving her room except to come for sessions with me, which she quickly terminated. Another isolated herself morally by silently singing to herself whenever she was in the presence of someone, thus preventing herself from hearing and understanding, and in this way she escaped any relationship. A third, a remarkably instructive case, was torn between dependence, love, hate and fear, and she combined relatively "reasonable" flight mechanisms with an *obsessional doubt bearing upon the existence of others and upon her own existence.* At other times she stopped taking her desires and fears for reality and limited herself to saying of her enemies that "it would be better if people like that did not exist." I should also point out in passing that this young lady possessed an intelligence that was only veiled by her affective troubles, and that she was

---

*These questions were examined during the spring session of the Société Suisse de Philosophie in 1977. There I presented for discussion some of the ideas proposed here. I have the distinct recollection of someone speaking of "phenomenology without reduction."

immediately very taken by the brief introduction to Descartes and Husserl that I gave her by way of reassurance. And it should also be noted that life for Descartes, Husserl, and Sartre was not always comfortable, the first secluded in his stuffy bed chamber, the second a product of the diaspora, ghettos, and pogroms, dying in the midst of the National Socialist persecution, and the third uprooted in a different kind of way, but one that was no less cruel... But once again let us not confuse philosophy with malady.

These defense mechanisms, be they neurotic, "psychotic," or even simply reactive, particularly the affective splitting of the ego, of the relation, and of the object, with all its consequences, are closely linked to what genetic epistemology calls the avatars, whether normal or pathological, of the intellectual synthesis and progressive knowledge of the "permanence of the object."[14] "And let the labouring bark climb hills of seas Olympus-high, and duck again as low as hell's from heaven!," cries Othello in the throes of his "complex," splitting his hatred from his love and with them Desdemona, successively called "the fountain from which my current runs" and "a cistern for foul toads to knot and gender in!"[15] There are two Desdemonas for Othello, one good and one evil, and the one disappears when the other appears. Here we have a synthesis failure, granted that Desdemona, with her harmless weakness for Cassio, of her own race, does not really change so abruptly and so totally as Othello imagines. In the same vein Popper relates an incident from the biography of Marie Ebner von Eschenbach. She recounted that as a child she used to fear that the world would disappear when she closed her eyes and would not reappear when she reopened them. Possibly a habit (apparently somewhat retarded) dating from the time when small infants abandon searching for the toy hidden under a handkerchief before their eyes? Or a defense mechanism? Perhaps Marie at some time in her life, with or without good reason, had been unsure of her mother's goodness, i.e., of a good mother who is always there or who always comes back.

There is another aspect of neuroses which will now command our attention: obsessive doubt (other than existential), verification, and perfectionism, which in their turn and perhaps in another way are capable of leading to the existential doubt. Further, these patients are often obsessed with the fear of "losing one's reason." Obsessive perfectionism is like the obverse of the greatest of human qualities, the desire for perfection. It is, if you will, a desire for the absolute which is mistaken in its object.[16] Now, as we shall see, "critical" philosophy, phenomenology in particular, rests deeply on the nostalgia or hope for an "absolute knowledge," relentlessly pursuing the least speck of doubt or possibility of doubt. I was therefore not surprised when I became aware of the relationship that Sartre made between psychasthenia (an obsessional neurosis) and the motives for a "serious" transcendental phenomenological reduction: "... not only do we have a coherent explanation for this trouble" (a painful "psychasthenic" phobia) "but in addition we have a permanent motive for performing the phenomenological reduction."[1] Perhaps it would be more correct to say that here we have two sides of the same coin. At any rate, that is what a phenomenologist should say. As for the obsessive fear of "losing one's reason," for now I will simply say that it is as rare, or rarely expressed, among "critical" philosophers as it is frequent among patients suffering from obsessional neurosis; often enough it is even one of the motives that prompts the latter to seek counselling.

Illusory impressions of unreality or of dreaming are observable as well in other mental illnesses, such as "psychoses" (a rather badly defined concept encompassing various neurotic processes as well) and epilepsy. We mention, among epileptic illusions, the impression of unreality known as the "dreamy state." It is not rare, and we would not be so imprudent as to deny that, like the "déjà vu" and "déjà vécu" impressions, it has given rise to certain philosopical positions.

As for oligophrenia, or intelligence deficiency, it is not included in the pathological thinking processes which I just described. It can, however, limit intelligence, and with it the development of the ego, which is the locus of the most advanced form of consciousness.

Let us now move on from fashion and illness as causes for a real or fictitious existential doubt and examine the properly philosophical motives for the "transcendental phenomenological reduction."

The desire for perfection, the quest for certainty, or for secure foundations on which to build,[9] the "search for an indubitable first principle,"[4] such is the touchstone of phenomenology, of what is called "critical" philosophy, and in a general way of all philosophy worthy of the name. It is another question why some either see or believe they see grounds for doubt, chiefly existential doubt, and thus pursue what in the minds of others—who do not see any ground for doubt—is a *"mistaken quest for certainty."*[9] With all the respect due to persons and particularly those "enamoured of the Absolute," even though we feel they err in the *modalities* of their quest, I wonder if we ought not make some additions to the common philosophical motives in the case of "critical" philosophy and phenomenology in particular, resembling a little the motives that we have just seen outside the domain of philosophy. I am thinking especially of obsessional doubt, impressions of unreality, of dreaming, and of a certain contempt for the world, whether justified or not—that so called "vale of tears"—and for "the flesh," i.e., for the less elevated aspects of the "carnal passions of the senses and the imagination," and even a disdain for our own proper consciousness or a considerable part of it, as in the case of certain oriental mystics who regard it as an illusory mirror of illusions... To which it would be well to add an amazing confidence in reason in general and in language in particular ("never to accept anything as true which I did not know as evident[17])," if only to enable them to make bad judgments about themselves. As for such surprising intellectual myopia among great thinkers that conducts them straight into such visible snares, such blatant sophisms and gross naïveties, perhaps therein lies a kind of local distortion of intelligence under the influence of the additional affective motives of which I was speaking. To put it briefly, these latter strike me as consisting in an *abnormal diminution of the instinct towards realism* and the sense of relation in certain people.

The transcendental phenomenological reduction.
Some of its difficulties.

The existential doubt, says Popper,[9] is irrefutable, for the doubter can always reply that perhaps he is dreaming. Some years ago I myself dreamt that I was discussing the theory of knowledge with a friend. My present intention is not to refute anything at all but, after having pointed out some possible parasitical motives, to underscore certain difficulties with the phenomenological reduction. These difficulties comfort the realist philosopher in his lack of "serious" motivation to execute the reduction, or better, in the patent impossibility of his doing so. I list a few of them: the impossibility of escaping from egology once entered; the inexorably progressive character of a "serious" reduction leading us irresistibly to a limit where either nothing or almost nothing remains; a certain logic inherent to the system, a kind of natural inclination within it, that leads some phenomenologists from putting existence between parentheses to denying it outright; the contradiction in using reason and language, which are entirely realistic, to deny realism; and the enormity of some of the pit-

falls, sophisms or naïveties, into which the phenomenologist rushes blindly with his head down, as the saying goes.

It is said that after Descartes trapped himself in egology he deluded himself in believing that he escaped from it by his "demonstration" based upon
the truthfulness of God, which he found at the heart of his own consciousness.[18, 2] In fact, one might wonder whether Descartes' first, basic, and
inescapable experience was one of something quite different and shared
commonly by all of us: the consciousness of a reality transcending him and
whose existence is beyond doubt; and whether his double illusion was
rather first to think that he could subject that existence to doubt and then,
despite its immediate evidence, to maintain that it could be reached only
indirectly by reflecting on consciousness. Perhaps Descartes foreshadowed
Heidegger in being ever the "shepherd of being," a moment disguised as a
phenomenologist. Husserl[10] reproaches Descartes for having missed the
transcendental phenomenological reduction. He himself seems to oscillate
between a repugnance to admit that he is a solipsist and the decision to persist in the "EPOKE," in the suspension of the judgment of existence, or the
impossibility of doing otherwise, an impossibility linked to the internal
exigencies of the system. Sartre, for his part,[1] clearly sees that the reduction implies solipsism, and that the latter endures as long as the former.

Moved by a desire for perfection which many of us share, but, in our
opinion, exaggerating the domain of what can be subjected to serious
doubt, Husserl excludes the existence of the world, his own body, and
even the bulk of his own consciousness from what he calls "apodictic,
adequate, certain, perfect, and total evidence"(!). It is such evidence
alone, according to him, which can serve as a valid foundation for philosophy. It is no less evident, as Popper remarked, not without humor, that as
a starting-platform it is much too narrow.[9] That base is even more narrow
than Popper thinks. It is even open to question whether it exists or, like
Balzac's *peau de chagrin,* it simply vanishes into nothingness to the
degree that, in faithfulness to itself and the spirit of the system, the reduction becomes increasingly radical. Sartre[1] reduces the "ego," the "I" of
Descartes and Husserl. The doubtful character, the "transcendence" of the
past which Husserl affirms, even when considered along with the possibility of thinking two things at the same time (actually observable under certain conditions and limitations), reduces Husserl's evidence to nothing but
the brief present of an amnestic lack of fixation. Even if we admit that
some certain evidence can be continually present, as Husserl's definition

requires, all that leads to it, accompanies it, or flows from it (notably the forty thousand pages written by Husserl) continually falls or re-falls into the doubt-filled past and, like in the myth of Sisyphus, must continually be recuperated and restored to the present... Thus, granted that it is possible to do so seriously, as soon as one inserts his finger into the gears of the transcendental phenomenological reduction, not only is it impossible to pull it out but there is no stopping until everything has passed on through, and there is little or nothing left that emerges from the other end of the machine. I have an inkling that this would have happened to Heidegger, that he would have reduced everything including phenomenology itself. After which he would have gone on to another approach to philosophy.[19] But I don't know Heidegger well enough to dare say so unequivocally. As for the confusion between being and appearance, this goes beyond the reduction properly so called, which consists exclusively in the suspension of any judgment about existence. But as I have said, between "acting as if something does not exist" and affirming that it does not exist, there is but a step or two, which some "philosophers" have not hesitated to take...including Winston Churchill's teasing cousins.

"It is knowledge which they (the sceptics) attacked, seeking within it weapons to turn back upon it," Callot tells us,[4] and that seems to me already quite noteworthy. "Rationality," adds Popper,[9] "language, description, argument, are all about some reality, and they address themselves to an audience..." That is by no means the least of the paradoxes of "critical" philosophy, about which vast numbers of works are entirely based upon the most ordinary language, the most common logic, and the most natural realism. To that suspicion of "contradiction," we might add some paralogisms such as the following: all certitude is conscious, therefore consciousness alone (or a small part of it) is certain. Zeno of Elea believed that he had demonstrated that Achilles could never catch the tortoise. But this has never stopped anyone from walking.

But before continuing on our way there remain some preliminary observations that ought to be made.

Apriorism.

Along with Kant, the apriorists have no doubt about the existence of the "thing in itself" but they believe that they are separated from it by the twofold opaque screen of the "a priori" forms and categories of their sensibility and their intelligence. It is consequently unknowable and—like the serpent that devours itself by its tail—knowing has no other object but itself. Nevertheless, the "rule of reason" coincides absolutely and "noumenally" with itself.[20]

I have discussed in detail this strange theory elsewhere.[2] I will limit myself for the present to three brief remarks. First, it appears that Husserl[10] had good reason to qualify the notion of the"thing in itself" as absurd: indeed, how could one fail to doubt, as does phenomenology, the existence of that which is avowedly unknowable? Second, apriorism seems to confuse knowledge with coincidence and to lock itself into the false alternative of "coinciding" (knowing, for the apriorists) or being cut off. For us knowledge is neither coincidence nor separation: it is a *relation,* and the most elementary psycho-physical experience shows us that there is an uninterrupted *passage* extending from the external stimulus to the most sophisticated states of consciousness: C is a function of B, B is a function of A, therefore C is a function of A. Finally—and this remark seems applicable to several forms of "critical" philosophy—there is, in a general way, *an error of one degree of reflection.*

Confusionism.

If knowledge, conscious knowledge, is not separation, if it is open to something other than itself, we ourselves are not thereby uninvolved in it, first by the very fact that it is a part of us. It is in this sense that Aristotle[21] saw in it the common act (we would prefer to say the common process) of an existent capable of knowing and one that is capable of being known. But this brings up a double difficulty: are we not really modifying what we propose to observe by our investigative procedures? And even if this is not the case how are the respective roles of the two factors in the "common process" delineated? Such questions, more than phenomenology and apriorism, but whose answers could lead to them, are of interest to a number of modern scientists and epistemologists. A certain type of responses has been well summarized by Bridgman, as quoted by Lorenz:[8] "The object of knowledge and the instrument of knowledge cannot legitimately be separated, but must be taken together as one whole." This is the sort of thinking for which I suggest the name *confusionism.*

Specialists in certain microphysical investigations[22, 23] remind us that there would be extreme cases in which the method of investigation used really modifies the object under observation in a way such that it is impossible to perceive anything but a resultant. The reason would be that the observation procedures are of the same nature and the same order of magnitude as the observed process. But without even envisaging the possibility of future progress in the study of elementary processes, from now on we have the cure at the level of statistics. Statistically speaking there is not the slightest doubt about what in those events of unfortunate memory was caused by the atomic bomb and what was caused by Nagasaki, Hiroshima and their unhappy inhabitants. As for basic responsibilities and what is permitted or forbidden during war time, these are other questions.

Analogous remarks can be made about other sciences and technics that actually modify. Take for example the case of psychoanalysis, and particularly psychoanalysis with a therapeutic purpose. It essentially seeks to *modify* the patient, i.e., to cure him. When successful the psychoanalyst can observe a true abridgement of individual evolution under the influence of the cure. This has never prevented any psychoanalyst from knowing which neurotic automatisms were at play before his intervention and what remained of them during the course of it.*[24]

We should add that certain methods of examination do not really modify: think for example of the "photographic safari," of observing wild animals from a long distance when the observer is concealed from their eyes and nostrils. Think of the medical diagnosis of measles or typhoid fever... Briefly, I think that the problem of observation that really modifies does not always exist. When it does appear it depends on the case and can require different solutions; even in difficult cases it is not necessarily insoluble.

The second difficulty can seem in some way more profound. Granted that we have not made use of investigative procedures that really modify their object, if knowledge is a process common to an existent capable of knowing and one that is capable of being known, then is it possible to distinguish the respective parts of each factor? And if it is impossible, then

---

Introspection is in no way that coincidence between non-reflective consciousness and itself by which the latter "is conscious of itself and of something other at the same time."[1] In my opinion it constitutes a technique of self study and, as such, belongs to the reflective consciousness. Does it modify the non-reflective consciousness when it scrutinizes it? Does it or does it not belong to methods that really modify? It seems to me that, paradoxically, it is rather when a state of non-reflective consciousness can be retained at the same time that "another part of ourselves" examines it, that its spontaneity is at risk. As for the psychological past, it is not modified. The present does not affect the past.

what does that definition of knowledge mean? What prevents us from regressing to apriorism, phenomenology, or solipsism? I indeed have had the feeling that Heisenberg sometimes wavered a little between these two positions.[23] In my opinion the solution to this problem is a simple one. It resides in the *multiplicity and variety of all the orders of witnesses,* which can belong to the "three kingdoms," animal, vegetable, and mineral, as well as to the world of machines, each in its own way making an identical judgment about the same event. If—as Newton apparently did in a moment of distraction—I fry my watch while checking the time on my egg, it is without the slightest "circle" that the egg, the watch, my guests, I myself and the cat, to say nothing of my cleaning woman tomorrow morning, will all be in general agreement about what happened.[2]

Consciousness as an illusory mirror of illusions.

Certain "mystics of the East" would suppress consciousness in themselves through ways other than suicide, sleep, or drugs. For them consciousness is an illusory mirror of illusions, a difference reflecting differences, and they turn away from it to seek *Nirvâna,* to dissolve themselves in the immanent, undifferentiated Center, of which the world and its variety of beings would be but distant and weakened emanations. At least this is what western religious and historians tell us. [6, 25]

This would not be the shadow of the eternal Ideas cast upon the wall of Plato's cave. It would not be the "dark night" of the mystics of the West, at once afflicted and supported by their faith, "a dark cloud illuminating the night,"[26, 27] nor would it be the contempt for the world of a certain kind of christianity pining after "paradise lost," believing that it is necessary to despise and turn away from creation in order to approach the Creator, and still less would it be that optimistic faith which maintains that "the Kingdom of God begins here below." And further, it would not be that modern, Hegelian-Marxist faith for which the Spirit—whether spiritual or material, if I may so speak—progressively discovers or rediscovers itself within History, Man, the State, the Party, the Philosopher, the Leader...[28] As for the law of differentiation-correlation-consciousness, which I feel underlies and marks the progress of history, this would be the worst illusion possible, since it is precisely *an illusory relation implying an illusory difference* that we ought to substitute for the fusion of differences within the Formless. Nevertheless, if such a way of thinking really exists it would be an error not to take it into account. Along with other spiritualities, its manifestation, perhaps the result of the atrocious "material" conditions in ancient India, would constitute an impressive warning against dispersive consumption: *mane, thecel, pharès...*

Other doubts about reason or its effectiveness.

In my younger days I had no existential doubt nor doubts about any, so to speak, "short term," "practical" value of my reason, but rather a doubt about my capacity, indeed the capacity of man himself, to solve the truly great problems, or even to pose them. To begin with, I had gone through disillusionment. As I put it then, I had "experienced the void," meaning for me that in respect to any *Weltanschauung* or deep knowledge of the world and myself I henceforth knew that I knew nothing, I knew not whether I could know, and "not knowing what I was I did not know what to want." I did not even know whether I was deceived by language and whether such thoughts made any sense at all. As I have said elsewhere,[2] perhaps events conspired with a certain natural disposition of mine to facilitate this kind of intellectual purgation. *Research* at least seemed justified to me, and I turned my life in that direction and still continue on the same course. Perhaps I am a little less ignorant than I was, but the surrounding night remains dark and I have a sense of a kind of attraction ahead, a kind of infinite depth...

Realism and realist criticism.

I note in passing that it was in *criticizing* certain aspects of critical philosophy that I began to sketch the realist position. For the realist there is no existential doubt, no separation, isolation, nor *a priori* circularity, no hopeless confusion between the two factors in the "common process" of an existent capable of knowing and one able to be known. At the very beginning of our voyage we spurn all naïveté and, with eyes wide open, recognizing the naïveté and artificiality of solipsism under all its forms, we cast off into the deep.

This is not to say that realist criticism is limited to this. It *disillusions,* casting out false certitudes as well as false uncertainties. It is neither too optimistic nor too pessimistic, and least of all is it without hope. It does not ignore our ignorance but does not take it as total and definitive. As a general and philosophical critique it has relationships of mutual support with the particular critiques inherent in the different sciences. In cooperation with them it scrutinizes the signs and conditions of truth—i.e., of the adaptation of the parts to each other and to the whole—of logic—ordered or not towards truth in so far as the postulates[29] or premises are true or false—of error, and of falsehood.

"Mental solipsism" and physiological reductionism. Inference of consciousness in others.

There is still another pitfall to avoid, what we might call a "partial transcendental phenomenological reduction," casting a doubt, if not denying it outright, on the consciousness of *the other*. This attitude, whether practical or theoretical, is not rare. It was that of Descartes, who had but recently escaped from egology, believed he had escaped, or had not yet truly entered it: for him animals, if not other human beings, were neither more or less than machines. This is the attitude of certain white colonists, industrialists, and "masters" of former times. It is still today that of a number of "physiologists of behavior" who maintain that they should and can explain the latter without taking into account consciousness, what Pavlov called the "fantastic and hypothetical" interior world of animals,[30] and even, as some American behaviorists think, the consciousness of their own peers. Freud was alluding to nascent behaviorism when he wrote "He thinks he can establish a psychology that does not take into account this fundamental fact (consciousness)."

I would like to take a brief moment to examine three questions. Why do the behaviorists imagine they should and can omit the consciousness of the other? What are the consequences of such a "reduction" on the study of behavior? Is it possible and necessary to infer that others are endowed with consciousness, or at least certain of them, and how does one go about it?

In my opinion the motives for attempting to work a "physiological reduction" ought to be sought in the conjunction of a legitimate desire for scientific rigor and an erroneous concept of knowledge, the same, in fact, that we have seen at work in "critical" philosophy (regardless of its less extreme character here): to know "absolutely" is to coincide; failure to coincide means irremediable separation. The inability to penetrate "to the interior of the other," the inability of living his very own states of consciousnes, is equivalent to the inability of knowing him, even his existence. We have seen that this is a misunderstanding of the nature of knowledge, which is neither coincidence nor separation, but relation, and that this applies as well to our reflection on our own consciousness. The most we can say is that our own non-reflective consciousness is "closer" to our reflective consciousness than that of others. Not only are the behaviorists deceived in believing they are obliged to omit the consciousness of the other, but there is also an illusion in the very thought of understanding a system capable of conscious relations without taking account of them. The most blatant consequence of the physiological reduction is a mistake about the correct level. The simplest approach for showing the possibility and necessity of inferring consciousness in the other is to give some examples. That is what I shall try to do now.

Inference consists in deducing, with greater or lesser necessity, from the likeness or analogy of other aspects, structures, or performances, a likeness or analogy of consciousness. This is also the way of the other natural sciences, and they too have differing degrees of certitude. I do exactly the same when I rely on symptoms to affirm the nature of the virus, the rotundity of the earth without having circumnavigated it, the existence of Edinburgh prior to being there, and my wife's presence in the next room when she calls me to dinner.

The least examination shows us that almost in its entirety our social life is grounded upon the implicit or explicit inference of consciousness in everybody. If this inference were to cease human society would disappear more completely and definitively than after an atomic catastrophe. Further, as I indicated previously, we have some reasons to suppose that a certain inferring of consciousness in the other is not entirely absent from a number of social, intra- and interspecific communications between numerous higher animals. If I whistle to my dog it is because I suppose that he hears and that he understands what I want of him. When a young ape that has been taught how to use sign language, and is able to perform at a level analogous to that of a five year old child, converses or corresponds with its teacher, is there not some kind of awareness of the consciousness of the other in both partners?[31, 32]

In certain sciences such as psychoanalysis, genetic epistemology, and psychophysiology the inference of consciousness in the other is perhaps no more general, profound, and obligating than in most human relationships, but it is more explicit and more precise. In its doctrine, aims, and application *psychoanalysis* is entirely grounded, theoretically and practically, on the inference of consciousness in the other and the distinction between what is conscious and what is unconscious, repressed, and which ought to become conscious during the cure. The psychoanalyst proceeds constantly to a double inference from the verbal account of the patient as to what he is conscious of in some way, and from that more or less vague consciousness to that of which he is not conscious. The monumental work of the *school of Piaget*, in which, as the saying goes, "the trees sometimes hide the forest," is centered entirely upon *interiorization*. It is the necessary condition of visual and verbal recall and anticipation, of reversibility, conservation, and of mental operations that are initially concrete and then formalized.[33, 34] There is a minor disagreement about the age at which interior visual images begin, with Piaget on one side and psychoanalysts such as Freud and Melanie Klein on the other. Genetic epistemology infers more archaic modalities preceding the start of interiorization, from as early as the "sensori-motor" stage. This discipline was initially applied to the study of human development but has now been extended to that of the ontogenetic and phylogenetic development of animals.[34] Somewhat like genetic epistemology, but with greater insistence placed on "neurophysiological" correspondences,[35] *psychophysiology* infers the existence and nature of interior, mental, conscious processes from certain behavioral structures and performances. If animals have eyes, ears, nerves, and a brain like ours, it is because, like us and at the same time in their own way, they see, hear, experience pleasure and pain, and think... And if they are capable of executing this or that performance, it is because they interiorize. Lorenz[8] estimates that no intellectually healthy person (with, we might add, a little familiarity with animals) can deny that they have a mental life. Pavlov,[30, 36] with a bit of self-contradiction, extends reflexology to the study of man's mental life. The latter, with the "second system of signalization" and inner speech, becomes capable of abstraction and generalization, i.e., of universality, to a degree and under modalities inaccessible to animals.

To return to spontaneous forms of inference of consciousness in the other, it is certain that this inference has no place in a certain number of social relations, among men as well as animals. This is the case when an "instinctual animal" reacts to a sign that can be isolated from its context, without any need to understand the latter, and, in the same fashion, when a newborn child exhibits a preadapted relational behavior such as *crying*, without having the least knowledge of the other and *a fortiori* of its consciousness; in a certain fashion it is the case when we relate to our own machines, robots, computers, etc., or, as I suggested a moment ago, when efforts are made to confuse us with them. It is still worth remembering that we do love cake and fear the rod.

CHAPTER II

Differentiation-Correlation-Consciousness

We have avoided some pitfalls: the existential doubt, phenomenological reduction, *a priori* separation, confusion between factors, solipsism, mental solipsism, and physiological reductionism. The road is clear and we can now push on. In the far distance we can scarcely see the "fusion of differences within the Formless." Henceforth consciousness can be recognized for what it is: an aspect characteristic of original, interrelated, and in a certain way expanding psychophysiological systems, which connotes the evolution of species, individuals, and civilization, in a word, of History, from a certain point of growth, throughout convergent, divergent, or contrary movements. This is what the law of *differentiation-correlation-consciousness* seeks to express, in which consciousness appears at once as a sign, consequence, and agent of differentiation and correlation, as a higher form of unity that implies, respects, and contributes to the originality of the parts.

Correlation: neither coincidence nor separation.

I must insist once again that relation, or correlation, is threatened from two directions. It vanishes with both coincidence and separation. It is coessential for a relation to be neither coincidence nor separation. What I said just a moment ago about knowledge, about "knowledge of something," even if that "something" is one's own non-reflective consciousness or the consciousness of others, is simply illustrative of this general characteristic of every relation particularized in one that is conscious. Non-reflective consciousness itself is perceived as relational and not as coincidence or solitude, as "consciousness of something" that is not itself and from which it is not separated.

First I will consider some particular approaches towards what very well seems to be a basic *law* of History, the law of differentiation-correlation-consciousness. I will then attempt to extract some more general considerations from these particular approaches.

The Darwinian approach.

"The branches (of the evolutionary tree)," writes Popper,[9] "represent later developments, many of which have, to use Spencer's terminology, differentiated into highly specialized forms each of which is so integrated that it can solve its particular difficulties, its problems of survival." He adds that "Darwin himself found Spencer's laws to be of little interest." Indeed, Darwin added two explanatory notions, those of *chance variation* and *natural selection through competition,* i.e., *the survival of the fittest.* Neo-darwinism has merely sharpened Darwin's notion of chance hereditary variation by assimilating it to some genetic mutations.[37]

Thus for Darwinism the genetic mutation differentiates and the competitive correlation chooses the mutant which has the best chance for survival and reproduction. The competitive correlation is at once the criterion and the agent of selection. It is fundamentally intraspecific, between individuals within the same species, but it also takes into account the quality of a broader reciprocal adaptation, e.g., the different capacities to pursue prey or avoid predators belonging to other species. Certain conditions lead it to act in a particularly powerful way, such as diminished territory and lack of food. To the extent that the learning faculty, intelligence, and along with them a higher consciousness, constitute an advantage in the *struggle for life,* they are at once a sign, a consequence, and (with chance variation) an agent of progress in differentiation and correlation.

This is not to say that other theories of the evolution of species cannot share certain of these views with Darwinism, or that Darwinism lacks difficulties. Among these latter figures the enormous volume of chance genetic variations required, which is the true "matter" of evolution, the *marble* thought to contain all that the *sculptor's* chisel, i.e., the competitive correlation which selects, will draw from it, and much more. In addition, the selection operates on actual behavior only, whereas the virtualities of the genetic types so chosen would be considerably greater. This discordance would be particularly impressive in our own species if modern man did not differ genetically from his Cro-Magnon ancestor. But it would also be possible among men as well as among drosophilae or bacteria for genetic mutations to occur over an extremely brief space of time and for genetic human types to go through transformations before our very eyes, so to speak.[37, 38, 39, 2] Let us add that Darwinian mechanisms explain or help explain the evolution of living organisms as well, such as plants, which are certainly not lacking in differentiations and correlations of differing kinds and degrees, but within which it is particularly difficult to infer a consciousness. Finally, at the other extreme, it is difficult not to see a certain tendency within the most spiritually evolved element of mankind to want to abolish Darwinian selection. Agriculturists and stock breeders simply use it and direct it. As for micro-surgeons, they dream of the day when they will be able to intervene directly at the genetic level. They have, as a matter of fact, begun to do so.

The psychophysiological approach.

Jackson maintained that for the evolution of both individuals and species, the thrust is from "the more simple to the more complex, from the more organized to the less organized, from the more automatic to the less automatic, from the less voluntary to the more voluntary."[40, 41] "Organization" is here understood in the sense of having few and relatively rigid connections, lacking in mobility, within simple psychophysiological systems with few nerve cells. Jackson was a neurologist, a psychiatrist, and, more particularly, he specialized in epilepsy. His teachings continue to dominate these disciplines. Later they were completed and rendered more precise by the notions of integration and subordination.[42, 43] They served as Teilhard de Chardin's inspiration for describing the law of "complexity-consciousness,"[6] or at least the first part of the law, which treats organisms and the evolution of species. He tried to extrapolate and to include the "body social" but this second part of the law of complexity-consciousness calls for some reservations.

Here the accent is on the internal differentiation and correlation, which are first considered under their anatomophysiological aspect, that of differentiation, of correlation, of intraorganic "complexification," particularly of nerve cells in terms of their number, of the quantity, quality, and the suppleness of their anatomical and functional connections. The psychophysiological hypothesis is postulated and verified, a subject I will be getting back to.[44] They are in very strict rapport with external correlation and differentiation. Perhaps more so than the latter they pose the problem of reality based analysis and synthesis, that of possible arbitrary separations within the "organic unity of the whole."[28] I will be reexamining this problem later.

Among the numerous psychophysiological methods there is one that seems to me particularly enlightening in respect to some of the questions being raised here. It is the method centered on *the study of elements common to the two aspects of psychophysiological processes, the mental and the anatomophysiological respectively.* Included among these common elements are time, repetition or non-repetition, the possibility or impossibility of simultaneity under the mode proper to each of the two aspects respectively, etc. Several years ago I had the occasion to develop this method and apply it in a variety of experimental studies which were recently published[2] in a less technical form than the original articles.* I offer an example, where the common element studied is *time.* Take t^0 as the origin of a time period, at which moment a visual stimulation is applied, such as colored light, a drawing, etc. At time t^1, after a few tenths of a second, an unconscious reaction can take place, such as a defensive, adapted blinking of the eyelids. A few tenths of a second later, at time t^2, gnosia, i.e., non-verbal recognition, occurs. Some tenths of a second still later, at time t^3, normally less than one second after the onset of visual stimulation, denomination takes place, either interiorly or expressed outwardly. It is possible to observe pathological increases of this or that period of time and a fleeting normalization brought about by a repetition of the stimulus.[45] It is possible to study in the same way the moment an image appears following verbal stimulation, as well as the occurrence of various mental operations. The moment at which the *modification of consciousness* takes place is signalized verbally or by a vocal or manual token. The *anatomophysiological aspect* consists in the excitement of neuronal systems at increasing distances from the sense organ, systems that are increasingly extensive and ever more complex. In respect to this

---

*See also "Consciousness and movement. Research on the motor component of inner speech and visual imagination, " contained in the present work.

last point, the intervals of time measured contain times of conduction and times of synapse. The use of repetition in reducing a time period originally expanded abnormally corresponds to an enhanced synaptic facility.

Let us note in passing that experiences of this kind do not merely permit us to "put our finger" on the psychophysiological *unity* of the process grasped under its two aspects, mental and anatomophysiological respectively. They allow us to spend some tenths of a second in assisting at a process, a growth, a *history* stretching from the most primitive adapted reactions—the fruit of the unconscious logic of the living being[46]—to the most sophisticated forms of consciousness and behavior. And we have some good reasons to think that here we have a kind of abbreviated analog of the evolution of individuals and of species, conforming to Haeckel's concept. Such experiences show us, as I have already indicated in my criticism of apriorism, that *there is no separation,* i.e., no airtight bulkheads truncating the process or cutting it off from the exterior stimulus foreign to the process itself. We can now add that this is valid for the process taken in its entirety, i.e., under both of its aspects: from both points of view, the anatomophysiological and the mental, the passageway is open and clear; if B is a function if A, and C of B, ultimately C is a function of A. *There is no more coincidence* between the two aspects, nor between either of them and the exterior stimulus. *But there are common elements,* and thus the *function* unites elements that are homogeneous. Furthermore, one can wonder whether this does not help sharpen the distinction we envisaged when discussing confusionism, between consciousness considered as act or process common to the existent capable of knowing and that which is capable of being known. If you will pardon me the truism, the common elements belong to both, and those that are not common distinguish them...

The genetic epistemological approach.

We have already noted that the School of Geneva has a double characteristic: it *infers consciousness* and assigns a central place within it to *interiorization.* The internal differentiation-correlation expresses itself in terms of successive *structures,* each one of which implies and surpasses the preceding one and is inseparable from the external differentiation-correlation. These successive "mental structures" depend upon hereditary virtualities which are themselves the legacy of the evolution of species, the fruit of *past relations*—and of *present relations.* The latter are progressively interiorized, and with the interiorization, a condition for mental operations, the child becomes capable of freeing itself from present concrete situations without thereby withdrawing from the rest of reality. Like all beings here below, it springs from relation, within relation, by and for relation. Logic issues from the truth, i.e., from the adaptation of parts among themselves and to the whole. It is fundamentally ordered to truth even though it can detach itself from it when, without losing its self-identity, it operates on the basis of erroneous premises or postulates. This is the very precise sense in which we must understand the expression sometimes used by Piaget:[47] "the construction of the real by the infant." He did not intend this to mean "the construction of the child by Piaget," independently of children...

Ethological and educational approaches, particularly reflexology.

Ethology is the study of animal behavior in a natural setting. Even though in principle its object is *innate behavior* as well as *learned behavior* it is in fact centered on the former. This is why it is well not to dissasociate it from the learning sciences, one of the most remarkable of which is reflexology. These two complementary sciences have been marked by such renown names as Darwin, Fabre, Huxley, Von Frisch, Tinbergen, Pavlov, and many others. My own former teacher, P.P. Grassé, has recently made some important contributions to the field.[48] From the perspective of differentiation-correlation-consciousness, I will limit myself to a succinct examination of the passage from innate behaviors to acquired ones, or, to put it better, of how the former fall under the control of the latter, initially in the evolution of species and then in that of individuals, particularly in child development.

Innate behaviors present a vivid contrast to learned behaviors. The individual receives the first whole and entire through the evolution of species. They are preadapted to the external circumstances in which the species has been formed. They can require an internal maturation of the organism but demand no learning whatsoever. They consist in adapted reactions to signs that can be isolated from a context which need not be understood. When the context changes, as for example under experimental conditions, the reaction persists but loses its sense of adaptation and the "stupidity" of the animal stands out. Learned behaviors, to the contrary, give evidence of its "intelligence." The two can lead us to infer the existence of mental processes, but with strongly different qualities. The two are formed within relation, by relation, and for relation, but in a certain fashion past relations dominate in the case of innate behaviors: we might call them "fossilized behaviors." With learning a great step forward takes place, in respect to relation, correlation, communication, and consciousness. The organism gradually acquires an increased ability to situate the parts in respect to each other and to the whole, within wholes of increasing breadth. Internal differentiation-correlation and external differentiation-correlation call upon each other mutually and grow in concert. One of the most remarkable differences highlighted by the improvement of relations is that of knowing, the difference in the capacity to learn. This difference intervenes powerfully in the selecting mechanisms which lead the evolution of species; perhaps it may reach such a point in our own species that these mechanisms would be bypassed, even directed, or abolished.[49, 50, 14]

This does not mean that learning behaviors abolish innate behaviors. They rather graft themselves onto the latter, prolonging and perfecting them in a process of *conservation and emergence*. We are a long way from knowing how many innate behaviors persist in man. We can at least affirm that pretty much all of the adapted behaviors of the new born belong to this category; conditioning and learning rapidly begin to take them under their control while at the same time previous and lower nerve structures submit themselves to higher ones, which mature anatomically and functionally later.[51, 52] Pavlovian conditioning is constructed entirely upon innate, unconditional, "absolute reflexes," such as the need for sustenance and for avoiding painful stimuli. Humankind itself, be it through the most sophisticated signs of signs and through the medium of the second system of signs, that of verbal symbols, is basically "in pursuit of its daily bread." [30] But we are dealing with the question of utilitarianism here, or of a certain disinterestedness and autonomy of knowledge, desire, action, and sense of beauty. I will return to this in my discussion of the psychoanalytical approach.

It is also important to understand that the capacity to learn has as much a genetic base as the most rigidly preadapted innate behaviors. Yet the explicitation of the genotype throughout the course of growth is more multivocal, being more a function of the milieu in the first case than in the second. The genetically defined functional structure allows an infinite diversity of functionings, i.e., of possible relations depending on circumstances; the instrument is more defined than the melodies; the brain more than what use is made of it (though, strictly speaking, the use and exercise

contribute to the anatomical development of the minute structures con-
necting neurones, and to the myelinization of axons).

The psychoanalytical approach.

Psychoanalysis regards living organism, especially man, as a complex of
past, present, and even envisaged, "projected," future relations. As Freud
himself reiterated in one of his last works,[53] his two successive "topics,"
the first of which centered on the distinction between the conscious and
the unconscious and the second on that between the Id, the Superego, and
the Ego, share some common ground. The Ego is at once the "place" of
the most advanced personal differentiation, of the most finely tuned correlations, i.e., reciprocal adaptation, and of the highest level of consciousness, directed by "the secondary process." This is not to say that the Id
and the Superego are entirely devoid of consciousness, nor that everything
within the Ego is conscious, as the Ego's unconscious defenses bear witness. Nor is it to say that the Id—the innate drives either modified or not
during growth—and the Superego are completely void of adaptive value,
no more than the "primary process," that "logic" of displacement, projection, introjection, splitting, etc., which dominates in the Id, the Superego,
the repressed unconscious, neuroses, and dreams.

Here as elsewhere, pathology helps us better understand the normal
process. As I usually explain to my patients, neurosis is "the sickness of
fixation and repetition." Both the cause and the effect of repression, affective fixation is accompanied by stagnation and regression, i.e., by the repetition of certain infantile attitudes which at one time may not have been
without a certain adaptive significance, but which has been lost with the
advance of age and the alteration of circumstances, to a point where they
become erroneous. The essential task of therapeutic psychoanalysis, or
analytical psychotherapy, is to help the patient break his old attachments,
which it does by the conjoint use of awakening consciousness and the
normalizing of the therapeutic relationship, sometimes incorrectly called
the "modification of transference." Then, when successful, the psychoanalyst can observe a kind of summary of evolution, of personal growth, of
Ego liberation and development, of expansion. In brief, an improvement
of differentiation-correlation-consciousness.

Humanity, Pavlov used to say, is out after its daily bread. But he added
elsewhere that "the mathematician tends towards truth as plants towards

light."[30] Freud himself maintained that our intelligence is fundamentally at the service of our primitive instincts, the drive towards self-preservation and the sex drive, centered respectively on the individual and the species. Initially he set them in opposition but later reunited them under the name EROS, or life drives, which together were opposed to the drive towards death, later called THANATOS. Psychoanalysis has made some progress since the time of its genial founder. One question currently under study in psychoanalytical circles has focused on the possible existence of an autonomous drive towards investigation, exploration, *relation,* admiration and "love," an "instinct towards realism" not coessentially ordered to the more intense and less dangerous satisfactions of the other instincts or directly derived from them by displacement or sublimation. One can even speculate whether this somehow disinterested interest drive, in a roughly drawn, embryonic way, is not at work within certain of our lesser brothers, or at least within the more evolved of them. To encourage rats to succeed under test conditions it is possible to reward them through the avoidance of an electric shock or by offering them a tasty delicacy or (and why not?) a nice young lady rat in heat. But experience shows that the gift of new objects to explore gives them a reward that is equally attractive.* [2, 14, 54] To be sure, all of this requires much careful examination and prudent interpretation.

Sociological, economic, and cultural approaches.

Society begins with *division of labor, specialization* among workers, and *cooperation* between specialized workers. Specialization excludes neither parasitism nor internal conflicts. Through its interior differentiations and correlations the "body social" can offer certain analogies with each of its individual constituent organisms. Comparison, however, is not reason, and the danger of erring about levels cautions us against taking this image too seriously.

Society would not exist without the individuals that compose it, but in a certain fashion it is more than the simple sum of them. To begin with, it is

---

*It seems to me that this is where the notion of the "spirit of adventure" ought to be situated, recently discussed by M. Jean-Louis Galay at the annual meeting of the Société Romande de Philosophie shortly before this article went to press. Is it an autonomous drive? Is it the displacement or sublimation of other drives, and, if so, which? The deep motives of those whom John Buchan called the "adventurers" are many, complex, often unconscious, and difficult to discern.

more durable than each of them taken individually and it is endowed with its own proper structures. This is one particular case of the theory of levels of the real recently reexamined by Hartmann,[55] where at each level, along with each new synthesis, one sees the sudden "epiphany"[8] of properties proper to the composite. The whole can have a *limiting* influence on its parts, masking and excluding certain of their potentialities: society imposes the division of labor, hence specialization; the molecule of water, as long as it exists, prevents its constituents hydrogen and oxygen from combining with other substances. But contrary to chemical composites, certain wholes *help* their parts, or even create them or assist in their creation: there is no society without men, but there are no men without a human society; society has a powerful action that forms and differentiates the individuals composing it and draws them into cooperation.

A few other points deserve attention here: the probable sporadic appearance of animal societies during the course of the evolution of species, without any direct filiation; the inference of consciousness within others in social relationships; "social memory," or civilization; the historical role of conflict or lack of conflict between different social groups; the role of internal conflicts, particularly those from the Marxist-Leninist and socialist points of view.

Biologists seem to agree on the lack of apparent direct filiation between different animal societies,[48] at least in those which exceed simple family association. Throughout the course of evolution animal societies would emerge from solitary species in a sporadic way. Resemblances probably proceed from a certain structural and functional analogy between individuals belonging to different species, and from certain exigencies common to all societies for a successful struggle for life, with possibly a limited number of solutions. In the same way, the differences would be sought among both specific differences and those of the milieu, particularly among the conditions in which competition and mutual assistance occur.

The question about the inference of consciousness within social relationships appears on two levels: the inference of consciousness within social individuals, and the inference of consciousness of the other by social individuals in their social relations. I have previously examined these two points. In respect to the first, I will do no more than point out again the excellent work of my friend Besuchet on the mushroom ant.[56] Like Lorenz, like "every mentally healthy person,"[8] Besuchet thinks they have eyes for seeing, sense organs for feeling, and, to account for the very extensive communication within the colony as well as for external relations, *at least* this elementary form of consciousness. More advanced studies, eventually applying methods of genetic epistemology to animals,[34] will doubtless one day show us the respective roles of learning and innate behavior in such societies, and the level of consciousness we are entitled to infer in their members. As for ants eventually inferring consciousness in other ants because of their social relationships, this is a much more difficult question. But I would not presume to say that it will remain forever unanswered. For the moment let us simply recall that the inference of consciousness within the other constitutes one of the foundations of our human society.

In human societies "social memory" holds a preponderant place, assured by oral tradition, pictorial arts, and writing, or the most modern and sophisticated means of information storage and diffusion. The invention of writing, followed by that of printing, constituted crucial moments for human growth. In a general way for certain among us a qualitative and quantitative increase in differentiation-correlation-consciousness can correspond to an increase in the goods of civilization and their diffusion. It is quite another sort of difference when a minority of the privileged, of "insiders," for one reason or another restricts access to these goods: it was perhaps deliberate on the part of some that megalithic civilization remained illiterate while the rest of the civilized world had long since learned to read and write. Not only can the vast majority be thus deprived of the common good, but the common good itself can be stripped of its nature, perverted, and used for inhuman ends. To any sort of "indexing," whether open, concealed, insidious, or violent, can be added the deliberate lie, whether by omission or by outright falsification, of various propagandas designed to turn us from what is essential. I will be returning shortly to these different or contrary movements.

If each has access to it, how is it that human culture produces differences among individuals? The issue is no longer that of a means used by the will to power and Darwinian selection to dominate or supplant others. Nor are we dealing with what one might call a competitionless narcissism: "to become all, desire to become nothing."[26] What is at issue is a greater *openness* towards the world, towards others and, in a way, towards oneself, an expansion of disinterested interest, admiration, and love for beings, for God as some of us believe God to be, for the Creator and his creatures, a *concelebration* as Catholics would say. The diversity of tastes, gifts, circumstances, and necessary specializations varies, nuances, and enriches the common tendency. Unification from the high is no longer to be sought or feared, for "the infinite depth before us" is more *unlimiting* than delimiting and, in that sense, identifying. In this movement we are progressively differentiated, and we distance ourselves in respect to the other living beings that have preceded us, our human ancestors, and our own past. Throughout the course of our analogous travels, at once varied and converging at infinity, each of us can contribute in ways both unique and common towards increasing the goods of civilization. These, according to Popper's *Objective Mind,* and *Third World,*[9] do not *sensu stricto* constitute a "collective consciousness," because, even in the case of the Freudian Superego, there is no consciousness except that of the individual. They transcend men, though men created them. No one can know them totally, but each is nourished by them, with the obligation to choose.

In closing this too brief social approach, I will cite three opinions with political overtones. For the *liberals* J. and J.-H. Pirenne,[57, 58, 59] civilization's progress is a function of the free movement of material goods because the latter is accompanied by the free movement of persons and ideas. First of all, the exchange and confrontation connote the external correlation between different social groups, with a heavy overtone of commerce: e.g., industrialized nations and those providing raw materials, laborers, and markets for manufactured products. Civilization begins with the sea. For *Marxism-Leninism,*[60, 61] the confrontation that drives progress is internal and violent: it is the class struggle. *Democratic socialism* in the Swedish manner tolerates and makes use of certain residues of private industrial capital and respects the will of the people as expressed in the ballot, would that will be to return to less "corrected" forms of liberal economics. It refuses to make the people happy despite themselves; the communists would say despite propaganda, obstruction, and adverse pressures. We add that certain Marxists are clearly deceived when they make civilization and the civilized consciousness mere superstructures, not to say "epiphenomena," of relationships based on production. But as Engels suggested in his letter to J. Bloch,[62] perhaps initially it may have been indispensable to stress the antithesis.

Differentiation-correlation-consciousness. Differing or contrary movements. Relations between the various movements.

These different approaches constitute so many points of view of a vast movement that is perceivable in History once a certain degree of growth has been achieved: the movement of differentiation-correlation-consciousness. Differentiation and consciousness are understood in different ways, first depending on whether or not they are interior to the organism or to the group. Both internal and external differentiation and correlation imply and elicit each other. Consciousness is a higher form of relating. The level of relation which consciousness signifies nuances it qualitatively and, so to speak, yields precision regarding its degree. As does every relation, it excludes coincidence and separation. In the law of differentiation-correlation-consciousness, it is at one and the same time a sign, a consequence, and an agent of differentiation and correlation, like a higher form of *unity* that implies, respects, and helps promote the *originality of the parts* and so constitutes a kind of tendency towards the *liberty of universality.*[2] As the latter progresses, consciousness increasingly relates each part to the others and to the whole, within wholes that are increasingly vast. The attraction exerted by the whole overcomes blind attachment to the part: "If you stop at some one thing, you do not cast yourself upon the All."[26] It is not an abstract, hollow universality relating to a universe absurdly devoid of contents and supposed to exist without the parts which compose it. It is not, as Christians would say, a hate or contempt for God's world as unworthy of us. It is the appreciation of each part in its relation to the whole, a rule of thought and action recommended as well by Mao Tse-Tung.[63] To put it briefly, it is a *concrete universality* involving all ways of knowing, acting, and loving, and the full range of qualitative nuances in our consciousness. This tendency towards concrete universality agrees with the diversity and consequently with the necessary modesty of approaches. This diversity constitutes an enrichment for all without excluding anyone from the common movement nor, within this movement, from grasping an essential in proportion to one's limits. In this sense it is true that everything belongs to all, an expression that aroused a modicum of the great Voltaire's raillery when he took it too literally...

The movement of differentiation-correlation-consciousness is not the only one to be observed in History. Among the different or contrary movements I would first cite the visible discordance between the progress of knowledge, particularly in the sciences and technology, and a certain stagnation in our intellectual and moral faculties, sometimes even frightening regressions. As Montaigne said, science then becomes a *science without consciousness* and could cause our ruin. I see at least a threefold

reason for this: our intellectual and moral growth is genetically programmed and limited in a narrower way than our learning possibilities;
the latter are in great part ordered towards the calculated satisfaction of
our "old instincts," as Freud emphasized so strongly in his last topic;[53, 64]
and, inversely, if we admit the existence of an autonomous exploratory
drive, it would be able to withdraw occasionally from the other drives,
and precisely from all the benefits and marvelous evolutionary preadapta-
tion of the "old instincts."[38, 65]

No less visible is the failure occurring in the development of consciousness stemming from an inadequate environment during childhood, and its
regression under the influence of a subsequent isolation. In *dreams* it is
external and internal isolation that leads to the illusion of perception (an
important apologetical motif of the existential doubt in philosophy) and
back to the "primary process"—that "logic" of condensation, displacement, projection, introjection, splitting, etc. which I spoke of in connection with the repressed unconscious and neurotic mechanisms. It leads as
well to faults less disguised than the preceding by superficial unity, the
apparent logic and truth of dreams: one who is dead yet lives, a woman
who is a lion, a bull or a cow, those curious "heautoscopies" in which one
views himself at a distance....[66] The regressions of adults who have suffered unfortunate isolation echo the psychological disasters of the premature and inadequate outplacement of infants, of the *hospitalism* described
by Spitz.[67] The wild man of Aveyron and the unfortunate sailors abandoned on Treasure Island and on The Mysterious Island are doubtless
closer to reality than Mowgli who so fascinated Baden Powell, or Robin-
son Crusoe. The latter, it is true, had quickly benefitted from the company
of Friday. *Escape from selective intra-specific competition* within
resource poor environments is without doubt one of the reasons why
archaic species persist along side more evolved species. Questions relative to the causes and effects of the *isolation of social groups,* to the
difficulties of communication between people, are particularly complex
and thorny; the general opinion is that they are ill-fated.[68] It would be
easy, alas, to multiply examples. The reader will have found some of them
in the preceding pages. Among the more tragic figure *denying people the
liberty of thought, information, expression, and culture.* Still more profoundly, *withdrawing information,* aging, stagnation, fixation and then
restriction of the field of interest, enfeeblement, and finally death counter,
or seem to counter, the vital movement of expanding information.

Among movements that are not opposed or contrary, but simply different, I will limit my references to the evolution of plants. These are good examples of a movement of differentiation-correlation, and, within that movement, a certain improvement of the "logic of the living."[46] But the structural and behavioral differences between them and us are such that, as far as our present knowledge allows, there is little to justify the inference of a vegetal consciousness.

The briefest glimpse at the evolution of species, the growth of individuals and social progress, shows us that on the whole the movement of differentiation-correlation-consciousness dominates. There is more here than the simple positive result of a kind of algebraic addition of positive and negative processes without any relation, where the former would prevail quantitatively over the latter. In a general way the different, opposed or contrary movements, are linked together organically. Life seems to need death in order to perpetuate itself and make progress: there is the case of Darwinian selection, of the carbon cycle—i.e., the food chain among living beings—of the place given to the young, etc. Consciousness doubtlessly began with the quest for pasture, the pursuit of prey and flight in the face of predators.[2] In the process of differentiation-correlation itself, the differentiation and the correlation, the unity and the diversity, are mutually responsive.[69]

At the risk of abusing the generous hospitality of "Conférences et Débats" I would like to add one more point before closing. It seems to me that in passing we have seen additional precision respectively in the notions of *real analysis and synthesis* and of *analysis and synthesis in the mind based upon reality*,[2] and that we have come to understand better the relations between ontology and history. Ontology is indeed the science of being as being. But one of the characteristics of being is to be one and many, permanent and changing. In a word, being is *historical*.

BIBLIOGRAPHY

1. J.-P. Sartre: *Transcendence of the Ego*. Hippocrene Books, New York, 1972.

2. Y. Chesni: *Dialectical Realism. Towards a Philosophy of Growth*. Translated from the French by J. P. Zenk, Palo Alto, Live Oak Press, 1987.

3. F. Martin, Y. Chesni: "Possibilité ou impossibilité de quelques processus simultanés ou concomitants avec divers éléments paroxystiques électroencephalographiques," Archives Suisses de Neurologie, Neurochirurgie et Psychiatrie, *96*, 2, 1965, 366-378.

4. E. Callot: *La philosophie instituée. La forme du savoir*. Marcel Rivière, Paris, 1977.

5. J.-C. Eccles: *Facing Reality*. Springer, New York, Heidelberg, Berlin, 1970.

6. P. Teilhard de Chardin: *Oeuvres complètes*. Le Seuil, Paris.

7. B. Brecht, *Galileo*. Grove Press, New York, 1966.

8. K. Lorenz: *Behind the Mirror: A Search for a Natural History of Human Knowledge*. Harcourt Brace, San Diego, 1978.

9. K. Popper: *Objective Knowledge. An Evolutionary Approach*. Oxford University Press, London, 1972.

10. E. Husserl: *Cartesian Meditations*. Martinus Nijhoff, Netherlands, 1988.

11. D. Christoff: *Husserl ou le retour aux choses*. Seghers, Paris, 1966.

12. *Studia Philosophica*. Annuaire de la Société Suisse de Philosophie. Vol.XXXVII, 1977, Verlag für Recht und Gesellschaft AG, Basel.

13. M. Klein, P. Heimann, S. Isaacs, J. Rivière: *Developments in Psychoanalysis*. Da Capo, Jersey City, 1982.

14. Y. Chesni: "Psychoanalysis and freedom," in the present work.

15. W. Shakespeare: *Othello*.

16. Y. Chesni: "Quelques problèmes à propos de la névrose obsessionelle," Archives Suisses de Neurologie, Neurochirurgie et Psychiatrie, *103*, 2, 1969, 428-432.

17. R. Descartes: *Discourse on Method*.

18. R. Descartes: *Metaphysical Meditations*.

19. P. Thévenaz: *What is Phenomenology?* Quadrangle Books, Chicago, 1962.

20. E. Kant: *Critique of Pure Reason*.

21. Aristotle: *De Anima*.

22. J.-M. Jauch: *Are Quanta Real? A Galilean Dialogue*. Indiana University Press, Bloomington, London, 1973.

23. W. Heisenberg: *Physics and Philosophy: The Revolution in Modern Science*. Torch Books, New York.

24. S. Freud: *The Complete Psychological Works*. Standard Edition. Norton, New York, 1976.

25. J.-A. Cuttat: *La rencontre des religions, avec une étude sur la spiritualité de l'Orient chrétien*. Aubier, Paris, 1957.

26. *The Complete Works of Saint John of the Cross*. Edited and translated by E. Allison Peers. The Newman Bookshop, Westminster, Maryland, 1945.

27. J. Maritain: *The Degrees of Knowledge*. Scribner, New York, 1959.

28. G.-W.-F. Hegel: *Phenomenology of Spirit*. Oxford University Press, New York, 1977.

29. E. Callot: *De la postulation en matière de philosophie*. Ophrys, Paris, 1970.

30. I. Pavlov: *Selected Works*. Foreign Languages Publishing House, Moscow, 1955.

31. R. Gardner, B. Gardner: *Communication with a Young Chimpanzee. Washoe's Vocabulary*. University of Nevada, Reno.

32. A. Premack, D. Premack: *Teaching Language to an Ape. Progress in Psychobiology*. Freeman, San Francisco, 1976, 333-340, 389.

33. J. Piaget, B. Inhelder: *Mental Imagery in the Child*. Basic Books, New York, 1971.

34. A. Etienne, R.-A. Hinde, J. Stevenson-Hinde: *Developmental Stages and Cognitive Structures as Determinants of What is Learned. Constraints on Learning*. Academic Press, New York, London, 1973, 371-395.

35. J. de Ajuriaguerra: "Neuropsychologie du développement." Leçons au Collège de France, 1976-1977.

36. I. Pavlov: *Psychiatry as an Auxiliary to the Physiology of the Cerebral Hemispheres*. Selected Works. Foreign Languages Publishing House, Moscow, 1955.

37. J. Monod: *Chance and Necessity*. Random House, New York, 1972.

38. K. Lorenz: *Die acht Todsünden der zivilisierten Menschheit*. Piper, München, 1974.

39. G. de Morsier: *Essai sur la genèse de la civilisation scientifique moderne*. Georg, Genève, Buchet-Chastel, Paris, 1965.

40. J.-H. Jackson: *Selected Writings*. Hodder and Stoughton, London, 1931.

41. Y. Chesni: "Petite contribution au centenaire de la théorie de Jackson," Revue d'Oto-Neuro-Ophtalmologie, *XLII*, 7, 1970, 416-422.

42. C. Sherrington: *The Integrative Action of the Nervous System*. New Haven, London, Yale University Press, 1947.

43. P. Mollaret, préface de L. Lapicque: *Interprétation du fonctionnement du système nerveux par la notion de subordination*. Masson, Paris, 1936.

44. J.-C. Eccles: *Brain and Conscious Experience*. Springer, Berlin, Heidelberg, New York, 1966.

45. Y. Chesni, F. Martin, H. Schaer: "Sur une malade souffrant d'aphasie avec augmentation variable de l'intervalle de temps compris entre le début des gnosies et le début respectivement de la conceptualisation et de la compréhension verbales. Notion de trouble fonctionnel systémique." Revue de Laryngologie, *87*, 3-4, 1966, 235-244, Portmann, Bordeaux.

46. F. Jacob: *La logique du vivant. Une histoire de l'hérédité*. Gallimard, Paris, 1970.

47. J. Piaget: *Construction of Reality in the Child*. Ballantine, New York, 1986.

48. P.-P. Grassé: *La vie des animaux*. Larousse, Paris, 1969.

49. C. Darwin: *The Origin of Species*.

50. C. Darwin: *The Descent of Man*.

51. André-Thomas, Y. Chesni, S. Saint-Anne Dargassies: *The Neurological Examination of the Infant*. Translated from the French and with preface by R.-C. Mac Keith, P.-E. Polani, E. Clayton-Jones, National Spastics Society and Heinemann, London, 1960. Out of print.

52. Y. Chesni: "Sur le cri et quelques autres comportements mimiques innés examinés pendant les premiers jours de la vie," Revue de Laryngologie, *91*, 5-6, 1970, 339-357, Portmann, Bordeaux.

53. S. Freud: *Outline of Psychoanalysis.* Edited and translated by Jas. Strachey, Norton, New York, 1970.

54. J.-L. Galay: Communication à la Société Romande de Philosophie, 1977, Revue de Théologie et de Philosophie, Lausanne, 1977-1978.

55. N. Hartmann: *Der Aufbau der realen Welt.* de Gruyter, Berlin, 1964.

56. C. Besuchet: "Les Atta, fourmis champignonnistes," Musée de Genève, *172,* février 1977, 2-11.

57. J.-H. Pirenne: *Les grands courants de l'histoire universelle.* La Baconnière, Neuchâtel, 1944-1956.

58. J.-H. Pirenne: *Panorama de l'histoire universelle.* La Baconnière, Neuchâtel, 1963. Out of print.

59. J.-H. Pirenne: *Le progrès collectif de la conscience individuelle.* La Baconnière, Neuchâtel, 1975.

60. K. Marx: *Das Kapital.*

61. V. Lenin: *Imperialism: The Highest Stage of Capitalism.* International Publications Co., New York, 1969.

62. F. Engels: *Ludwig Feuerbach and the End of Classical German Philosophy.* U.S.S.R., Los Angeles, Progress Publications, 1969.

63. Mao Tse-Tung: *Selected Works.* Foreign Language Publications, Pekin, 1982.

64. S. Freud: *The Complete Psychological Works,* Standard Edition. Norton, New York, 1976.

65. Vercors: *Les animaux dénaturés.* Albin Michel, Paris, 1952.

66. Y. Chesni: "Quelques remarques sur les rêves dans leurs rapports avec la théorie de la connaissance," Revue d'Oto-Neuro-Ophthalmologie, *XL,* 7, 1968, 361-366.

67. R. Spitz & W. Godfrey Cobliner: *First Year of Life: a Psychoanalytic Study of Normal and Deviant Development of Object Relations.* International Universities Press, Madison, Ct., 1966.

68. T.-A. Lambo: *Communication Between Individuals and Between Nations. Getting the Message Across, an Inquiry into Success and Failures of Cross-Cultural Communication in the Contemporary World.* The Unesco Press, 1975.

69. D. de Rougemont: *L'un et le divers ou la Cité européenne.* La Baconnière, Neuchâtel, 1970.

PART TWO

*Psychoanalysis and Freedom**

*Conference delivered February 26, 1975, at the
Cercle d'Etudes Philosophiques d'Annecy
(Conférence et Débats, 1, 1975).

It is with joy that I have agreed to deliver a conference before the members of the *Cercle d'Etudes Philosophiques d'Annecy,* under the patronage of the *Académie Florimontane,* and it is with a certain apprehension that I have chosen its subject.

Annecy is thrice dear to me. City of spiritual struggles, with St. Francis de Sales, St. Jeanne de Chantal and Philothea. City of the Resistance, near the *Plateau des Glières.* The region where my refugee family found welcome during the occupation. I myself was in the *Sanatorium des Etudiants de France,* at Saint-Hilaire-du-Touvet, close by the Grande-Chartreuse. In a way it had already been quite some time since I had passed the health exam given me by my cousin Monteux at the *Ecole de Saint-Cyr,* in order to begin my medical studies in the French Navy. At the moment I was "resisting" Koch's bacillus and preparing for other voyages and other struggles.

"Psychoanalysis and Freedom." In my opinion this is a subject of considerable theoretical and practical interest, as well as vast and difficult. More than by the limits of time and space, the difficulty is augmented by the happy diversity of the public, in contrast with a certain tendency of psychoanalysis, at least of "chapel psychoanalysis," to turn inward upon itself. I will try to be as brief as possible, to avoid technicality and the esoteric without sacrificing truth. My subject is our tendency towards *freedom,* some of the pathological barriers to that human growth, that increase in consciousness, as well as the meaning, diagnosis, prevention, and resolution of these obstacles within an open, advanced psychoanalytical perspective. I beg the indulgence of my audience, and I hope a discussion will ensue.

Zoologists tell us that once a male robin has matured sexually, during mating season it is powerless to avoid attacking another male robin, with all the signs of what we, through a relatively safe intersubjective analogy, would tend to call "fury." But it expends the same fury on any bit of red stuff outside of context, like a few feathers or a bit of material. These combats between males doubtlessly offer the greatest biological interest, charging as they do the most able, the strongest, the bearers of genetic superiority with the task of perpetuating and improving the species. But even though its behavior is useful and adapted, and in that sense logical and true, the animal does not know what it is doing. It is probably not even conscious of sexual rivalry: a bit of red material is not something to be jealous about. The totality of the situation escapes it, and with it the meaning of the triggering sign and the triggered reaction. It reacts to the sign compulsively, without understanding. It is a prisoner of the sign.

We ourselves often react in the same way, and sometimes it is well that we do so: there are some circumstances, some moments when it would be inopportune, even dangerous, to think, when it is better to let our reflexes take over, be they innate reactions, acquired habits, or obedience to authority. But what singles us out as men and women is the possibility of not becoming blinded or bound by a detail, of understanding the whole, of locating the parts in their relations with each other and with wholes of increasing breadth: the liberty of universality, concrete, correlative with growth in relationship with oneself, others, the rest of the world, and even with God, according to the beliefs of some among us; correlative, as the Hegelians, Marxists, and other philosophers maintain, with a progressive awakening of the whole within the part, of reality within man, the apex of evolution and revolutions, mirror of the universe or image of God.

My lecture will be divided into two parts. In the first I will deal with innate or learned reactions to signs where there is no understanding of the whole, and then with growth in consciousness and freedom. The second part will be devoted to neurotic obstacles to that growth, and to the mechanisms, diagnosis, treatment, and prevention of neuroses. Based upon psychoanalytical examples touched on in part one, along with other biological and social examples, I will add a summary note on the meaning and importance of conflicts in the progress, stagnation, or regression of consciousness and freedom.

CHAPTER III

Innate and Learned Automatisms. Growth in Consciousness and Freedom

A. INNATE AUTOMATISMS

Innate behaviors are bestowed upon the new organism whole and entire through the prior evolution of the species. They require no learning. Some of them are manifested from birth, and others appear later after an internal maturation. As in the case of the robin, they consist in "automatic" reactions to signs which can be isolated from their context. These latter require no understanding.

Some examples of innate automatisms in the new-born human.[1,2]

Aside from some possible limited learning *in utero,* greatly reduced necessarily because of the foetus' situation and his weak cerebral development, the behavior of the new-born human being is principally innate, a heritage from its animal ancestors. I offer some examples quite familiar to mothers, nurses, and pediatricians, sometimes less so to psychologists, psychiatrists, and psychoanalysts. The reaction of "searching," leading to the discovery of the nipple. The "cardinal points" reaction in which the tongue, lips, and head incline in the direction of a light tactile stimulation of the labial commissure or of the upper or lower lips. The turning away of the head when the ear is rubbed, or when subjected to an intense light. The orientation of the head and eyes towards a soft light. The eyes that follow the motion of a shining or otherwise contrasted object. A slight frown mounting to a howl of rage—the existence of a progression, of transitional states, is noteworthy for psychoanalysis—driven by hunger or various bodily excitations which the adult will later describe as disagreeable or painful. The "satisfied smile" that follows sucking, before burping. Mandible movement seemingly without reason, perhaps sucking activity, and smiling during half-sleep. Thumb sucking already observable *in utero,* which is difficult to look upon as an auto-erotic substitute for sucking the breast or the bottle, or even for the deglutition of the inexhaustible bounty of the amniotic fluid. The grasping of the fingers and toes, posture reflexes, various movements of the body and its various segments, the major organic reactions associated with feeding, respiration, and excretion, mechanisms which assure the passage from placental life to an aerial environment: such are but a few of the innumerable kinds of innate behavior, many of them already existing before the time of birth, which help assure the survival and development of the child. André-Thomas called them "primary reactions," making them the behavioral aspect whose neurophysiological counterpart is predominantly sub-cortical, the cerebral cortex for the most part being still non functional at that age. Some details can be clarified in anatomo-clinical comparison, thanks to the maps of neuro-anatomical development that we now have at our disposal. Among others the excellent works of Leroy-Conel and my friend Rabinowicz of the Minkowski School at Paris and Zurich come to mind.[3]

Other examples of innate automatisms in animals and man, and at other levels of development.

Remember that certain innate behaviors can manifest themselves for the first time long after birth, for the same reason that some of them can appear before birth: it depends on the degree to which the organism has matured internally. Remember also that they can differ strongly between species, and that some of them can be replaced by learned behaviors in more intelligent species. Thus intra-specific aggression appears to be an innate behavior in the majority of species, among others in our own, but the inhibition of that aggression, equally innate in a number of species (e.g., predators that have strong "natural" weapons), ceases to be so in other species such as ours and is replaced by inhibitions of another nature, especially socio-cultural ones. And recall finally that similar innate behaviors do not necessarily imply a direct phylogenetic filiation, but that, the same necessities producing the same effects, they may arise from what is called a "parallel evolution."

The innate prestations between sexual partners, and between parents and children have been abundantly described. Their usefulness for the conservation of the species, i.e., sexual filiation, is particularly clear, and it is always surprising to see biologists hesitate to classify as sexual, in the wide sense, the breast feeding of offspring! Whatever, these behaviors, in different ways, are more or less linked to a series of other behaviors that are no less innate and fundamental for the survival, growth, and progress of the individual, the group, and the species: the quest for nourishment, inter- and intra-specific aggression, flight, habitation, hygiene—licking, delousing, purifying the soil, burying fecal matter, disposing of the dead—a service behavior that goes totally beyond family relations, sometimes even those of the group and species, and others that are linked to territory, hierarchy, etc. We have some reasons to think that a number of these innate automatisms exist in our species and that they have been wrongly attributed, or at least in an overly exclusive fashion, to experience, education, instruction, learning, and, in a general way, to socio-cultural influences. But here we have lands still largely unexplored.

Aggression and its advantages.
"The sacred shudder." The "Abraham complex."

Lorenz seems to have wanted to reduce Freud's "death wish" to intra-specific aggression and its derivatives; we will have the occasion to examine this in greater detail. In the true spirit of Darwin he insists on the importance of this innate instinct for the conservation and evolution of the species, up to a certain point where it becomes necessary for inhibitions to intervene in order to protect the latter from self-destruction. Changes occur in goals, in objects, in the "external pole of aggressiveness," resulting in new functions that are no less and no more useful to the individual, group, and species than the residual primitive drive, to the point of becoming the very base, condition, and expression of the bond of love: "being together against the other...," being able to unite in true or simulated struggles against real or imaginary enemies, in military parades, in triumphant displays... Once again we must note the similarity in processes observed in the evolution of species and in individual learning, here the processes of displacement, sublimation, etc. In our species learning clearly intervenes, but there is general agreement in thinking that aggressiveness is equally "innate."[4]

Who among us has not experienced at one time or another the vestigial reaction of the "sacred shudder," the neuro-motor part of which, namely the pilo-motor reflex, recalls the ancestral bristling of the hair, an apparent increase in bodily bulk designed to frighten the enemy? Lorenz tells us that, for this reaction to occur, the following stimulations must coincide: the defense of the group or of a group (or even universal) value against a menacing enemy, preferably within a group, a crowd, and under the command of a leader. "One people, one faith, one Führer...," a martial or religious refrain, the Ninth Symphony, a feeling of exaltation. The triggering signs themselves are certainly subject to education, and demagogues are not alone in their ability to use the militant enthusiasm of *Begeisterung*.

And we who are psychiatrists or psychoanalysts, how many times have we tried in our counseling sessions to console or cure mothers who are terrified and guilty about their desire to kill their own children or, what often amounts to the same thing, their fear of having the irresistible desire to do so... Remember that intra-specific aggression is probably innate, and that in our species its instinctual inhibition is weak or absent. If Abraham was deceived in attributing to God the order to kill his child, or if he was mistaken about the order, or if in accord with sacred history God was satisfied in putting Abraham to the test in the full knowledge that infanticide was not impossible, thus prefiguring the sacrifice of Christ, we are obliged to wonder whether Abraham's initial project, or simply its possibility, revealed no more than a religious injunction. Furthermore, all of this deters us from considering the fear children have in the face of terrifying parental *imagos* as nothing more than the unconscious projection onto the other of their own aggressiveness. Often there is probably more true objectivity in these imaginings than is generally admitted.

Attachment, detachment, the instinct towards relationship.

At this time ethologists and psychologists make much of what they call "attachment," which they consider an innate instinct, exhibiting early manifestations[5]. Harlow shows us that the very young baboon prefers contact with a warm piece of fur to sucking on a bottle of milk. This somewhat reverses the Freudian idea—at least as far as the baboon is concerned—that the mother's first fundamental prestation towards its infant is of the alimentary order, and that the sexual libido and the partial oral drive, the objectal or narcissistic satisfactions linked to the oral erogenous zone, will develop by an anaclitic connection with alimentary auto-conservation in consequence of the supplementary pleasure connected to it. The foetus' thumb sucking *in utero* has already introduced some doubt or precision. Spitz is perhaps less successful in analyzing it when he describes, under the name of "hospitalism," the disasterous effects of premature separation of the child from its mother. Independently of Harlow but in agreement with him, Bowlby shows that there is a multiplicitly of factors, of "independent variables," or better described as more or less independent variables, in the primary attachment of the infant for its mother, without forgetting the differences between the human infant and the young ape. Particularly important is the greater length of time needed for postnatal development in our species.

Harlow, Bowlby, and Zazzo insist on the fact that the attachment, the relationship to the other, is initially "autonomous," not "utilitarian" or at least not grounded in the satisfaction of other needs like eating, except perhaps for those of physical contact and warmth after the baby's expulsion from the womb, and—who knows?—perhaps some ingrained feeling of nostalgia for it. I myself made an analogous observation about the Ego's development and a certain insufficiency of Feud's second topic to account for it. I will come back to this for a longer look, but for now I merely suggest that the exploratory activity of the young ape and the human infant, its correlations with the mother's distancing and its probable relative autonomy, should be examined in an analogous perspective. Here again, and on numerous levels, we have *terrae incognitae*, and it is not at all certain that our own exploratory activity as passionate adult observers signifies no more than sublimated desires for wealth, sex, combat, admiration, domination, and even immortality.

Innate behaviors characterized as fundamentally realistic, "objectal," adapted and in a certain way logical and true but ultra-analytical. "The wonders of animal instinct and animal stupidity." Darwin's theory and two difficulties with it.

Without thereby minimizing the Ego's adaptive role for present reality in species where learning predominates, innate behaviors are generally considered to be formed equally in, by and for relations, and that consequently they also are realistic, "objectal," coessentially ordered to reciprocal adaptation, to the best reciprocal adaptation, and in this sense logical and true.[6] But the innate triggering signs are extraordinarily analytical, in a sense "abstract." It is the color red that provokes the aggression of the robin, and the yellow interior of a widely gaping beak that triggers regurgitation and the feeding of the young among various birds. These signs are chosen by evolution after the model of the key and the lock: they must usually, if not always, happen in *ad hoc* situations, at the risk of seeing the reaction frequently triggered inappropriately, causing more serious harm to the animal.

Nevertheless, under certain circumstances these signs can be separated from their "natural" context, as when hunters use particularly stylized lures, or in experimental artifices. The animal's lack of intelligence then shows itself to its full extent, in contrast with its marvelous instinct. Here is another example. The chirping of its young inhibits intra-specific aggressiveness among geese and triggers parental behavior. This is why a deaf goose kills its young, while one with hearing lavishes its attentions on rude decoys which conceal microphones emitting the recorded chirping of goslings.

The classic Darwinian theory, under its old form as well as its modern one, both mutationist and molecular,[7] accounts for these facts fairly well. The two "Big Constructors," in the words of Lorenz, or the material, formal, efficient, exemplary and final causes as the Ancients would have said, are partly variation, genetic change purely and simply by chance, and partly natural selection based upon the single criterion of the need for reciprocal adaptation at its best. Change that is purely and simply due to chance, is, if you will, the marble; the choice of the fittest (in the sense of reciprocal adaptation) is at one and the same time the project, the model, the chisel, and the act of the sculptor. One possible difficulty is the breadth demanded by chance variation, a difficulty increased by parallel evolutions. Another, perhaps more a visible one, offered by experiencing and reflecting upon behaviors, is the fact that natural selection bears only on the part of genetic virtualities that have been effectively realized. The latter represents, particularly in our own species, the merest fraction of further realizations. Finally, the Darwinian theory does not pose the question of the origin of a more or less "first" matter, so called, and submitted to the double law of chance and necessity.

The complexity, sophistication, adaptive finesse, and the already rather synthetic character of the "great parliament of instincts." Interactions between reactions. Displacement of the external poles of the drives. A note concerning reactions that lack triggering signs.

We should not believe that the innate instinctual behaviors of those animals in which they predominate leave them, in comparison to learned behaviors, gross and clumsy automata. In fact they correspond to very complex, sophisticated ways of being, ways that are finely adapted under ordinary circumstances, those in which they took their form throughout the course of the evolution of species. Two mechanisms contribute to this: the interactions between reactions, and changes in objects.

Among the first of these let us cite conflicts between two drives that are somehow opposed. These can result in contradictory movements, apparent immobility, compromise or equilibrium solutions, etc. When a newborn baby has its ear rubbed rather vigorously while the corner of its mouth is being gently stimulated, it reacts by turning its head away and drawing its lips and tongue towards the gentle stimulation. Two little fish, who stake claims to territory, determine their common border by the same composition of forces, behaving more aggressively the closer they are to the center of their domain, and more timidly and poised for flight the further they are from it; at the border, in a situation of equilibrium between aggression and flight, one can, so it appears, observe that in the same animal some of the fins are pushing forward while some are pushing backward. We have glimpsed other examples of conflict between innate reactions with the instinctual inhibition of murder among one's own kind: the peeping of goslings, an infantile or female behavior, a gesture of begging for food, the offering of the throat to the adversary's jaws, etc. We do not know whether the gesture of offering the rump to the leader in simulated coitus as a sign of appeasement is innate or learned among apes, like their way of mutual tickling to make each other laugh. Be that as it may, let us note that this wide variety of interacting instincts, this great "parliament of the instincts" in the words of Lorenz, constitutes the somewhat synthetic counterpart to the ultra-analytical character of each one taken separately: reality, as it were, is viewed through a prism. It remains an open question whether our own analyses of the "different instincts" are as well founded in reality as are, in a way, what we call the unity of the subject and that of the milieu to which it reacts. I will not here go into this general problem of the theory of knowledge but simply point out that the notion of independent variables can be useful.

Nor will I go further into changes, displacements, and object sublimations that take place throughout the course of the evolution of species. To the few examples which I have already given can be added that of the gull tearing furiously at bits of foliage as a substitute for the feathers or eyes of its neighbor, which is both its ally and its enemy. Let us simply recall that analogous processes are observed throughout the development of the individual, leading to, among other examples, rugby packs and the Olympic Games. As for the "empty reactions" of which Lorenz speaks, these would show an irresistible tendency towards instinctive realization not only by means of *ersatz* or more validly sublimated goals and objects, but in the absence of any "exterior object" as well. The affirmation of their existence requires great prudence: to limit ourselves to this example, how can we be sure that an orgasm, a nocturnal pollution, was not the consequence of a forgotten contact, touch, or dream?

B. ACQUIRED AUTOMATISMS

Certain learned reactions can take on an analogous character of partial, rigid, and forced automatisms that do not necessarily involve an understanding of the whole situation. I will devote less time to it for it treats of facts that are better known, particularly by psychoanalysts.

We cite "imprinting," as described by the ethologists, privileged moments of initial development in which, in certain species, exterior impressions become fixed in a prevailing and quasi indelible fashion. There is, for example, the gosling that saw Lorenz upon hatching and thereafter considered him to be its one and only family and remained unable to rejoin its own species. We know of nothing identical in man: even neurotic fixations can be cured, even values, or the so-called values chosen by the adolescent as the object of his *Begeisterung,* of his militant enthusiasm, can be changed, no matter how often this is accomplished only with great difficulty, if later his experience, his reason, or simply overwhelmingly or insidiously constraining circumstances demand it. As far as we know age is no limit to personal upheavals, even brain washings, deconditionings or reconditionings, and self-criticisms of all kinds.

We cite the mnemonic traces, whose nature and location are still so mysterious, traces often persisting and resisting change as long as they persist, though not always able to be remembered under ordinary circumstances. These traces form the base for normal memory, as well as that of those special recollections that can invade consciousness in a forced, involuntary, coercive, repetitive, "stereotyped" way during certain epileptic crises, or when an electric stimulus is, in neurosurgery, repeatedly applied to the same location of one or the other of the brain's two temporal lobes; Pennfield calls such recollections flashbacks, or experiential responses.[8] It was during one of these crises that a patient of mine, an adult at the time, kept seeing herself as a young factory worker of thirteen clad in a Scotch apron; another used to see a woman, always the same one, who spoke to her reassuringly… Later I will return to the subject of mixed crises, i.e., those which are alternatively epileptic and neurotic.

We cite what we call "habits," good or bad ones, which are followed without thinking, and which are so difficult to break. As for Pavlov's conditional reflexes, even though they have to do essentially with temporary connections, under certain conditions and among animals of a certain type, they can be extremely durable: this is the case with animals having a "strong" and "inert" constitution, and when excitations have "collided" or been too intense.

C. GROWTH OF CONSCIOUSNESS AND LIBERTY

The innate and learned automatisms constitute the basic structure, the framework, as it were, and underpinning of later developments in the direction of a greater flexibility, coherence, and comprehension. It is another kind of reciprocal adaptation that is now developing, increasingly conscious, intelligent, synthetic, ever better able to understand the whole, increasingly free, and if, like Jackson, we understand the word to mean something narrow and rigid, increasingly less "automatic." This second modality of logic and truth does not exclude the first, nor is it opposed to it. It builds upon it, assumes, penetrates, exhausts, and goes beyond it. So, without thereby losing its proper originality, living being, man, begins a more vast and profound dialog with the whole of reality.[9]

Some modern approaches:
"experimental psychology," reflexology, psychoanalysis.*[10]

Experimental psychology, better called the physiology of behavior, with the exception of Pavlovian reflexology, makes frequent use of puzzle boxes. These show that higher animals proceed gropingly at first, by trial and error, but that they eventually disengage some general laws and apply them at once, without hesitation, to the solution of new problems of the same order.

Pavlovian reflexology shows us that "signs of signs" and the second system of signalization, i.e., verbal signs or their equivalents, yield little by little to abstraction and generalization, to the universalizing, in a sense, of conditional reactions.

Psychoanalysis, at least after Freud's "second topic,"[11] shows us the three "agencies," the Id, the Ego, and the Superego pitted against each other; Eros and the "libido," neither of which are exclusively sexual, against Thanatos and the "destrudo" or destructivity; the "life instinct" against the "death instinct"; the instinct for self-preservation against the sexual libido, ordered towards the perpetuation of the species; the narcissistic libido against the objectal libido; the partial drives against the integrated drive; the pleasure principle against that of reality; the more or less subjective "imagos" against objective truth; exterior, interior or interiorized conflicts, the "anaclisis," mutual help, oppositions, struggles, conciliations, subterfuges, and victories that undergird, promote, and signify the development and blossoming of persons.

For Freud the Id is a mixture of innate behaviors and early, precociously repressed experiences; it is not totally unconscious for the main reason that it is subject to the pleasure principle; it is, nevertheless, the least conscious of the three agencies.

---

*My plan of exposition constrains me to postpone treating progressive synthesis according to post-Freudian psychoanalysis and Piaget, its rhythms, delays, repetitions, regressions, and shiftings. But I must express my thanks at this point to my very good friend Andrée Désailloud. Her expertise in genetic epistemology and in affective psychology has been most valuable for me in the conception and focus of several parts of this work.

The Superego is the collectivity of the great commandments, the great socio-cultural taboos to the extent that the individual makes them his own without being aware of it. "Thou shalt not kill"—and particularly thy parents, thy children, and thy fellow tribe members. "Thou shalt not fornicate"—above all with thy father, mother, son, daughter, and the wife of thy friend and ally, at least not without his consent. Let us note in passing that in a number of animal species the respectively parental and genital behaviors are generally exclusive of one another; it is not certain whether such an instinctual obligation does not intervene equally in our own species, along side the obligation of openness for the biological family and of alliances by means of the "exchange of females," which modern ethnologists consider the principal reason for the generalized taboo against incest. Let us also note that no matter what may be the degree of sexual permissiveness in a society, the simple requirements of maturation, questions of anatomical dimensions aside, continue to militate against incest, and thereby in a way impose the Oedipus complex. This appears to escape many "emancipated" people, or those so called, who think they can do away with "sexual problems" by admitting general license; to say the least, the latter is physiologically impossible.

Finally, the Ego is described by Freud as the most evolved and conscious organ of adaptation to reality. It plays the role of arbiter between the Id, the Superego, and present reality, seeking an ever increasing reciprocal adaptation. It is the great calculator, aiming to obtain the maximum of pleasure with the minimum of displeasure, the minimum of bother. Less so than Superego, and especially less than the Id, it remains partly unconscious, as certain unconscious Ego defenses bear witness.

Utilitarianism or autonomy of certain modalities of relations and of a certain Ego progress.

A tendency of thought, observable in experimental psychology as well as in reflexology, ethology, and psychoanalysis, consists in ordering all progress, that of individuals and that of species, towards ever improving the satisfaction of the primordial instincts, such as those of self-preservation and those associated with the perpetuation of the species, taking into account the demands of exterior reality and particularly those of the social context.

Ethology and psychoanalysis refine these untilitarian perspectives by the notion of derivation: it happens that the source, the "internal pole of the drives," remains unchanged throughout the evolution of species as well as that of individuals, while the goals, the objects, the "external pole of the drives" change through reorientation, displacement, and sublimation.

Finally, certain psychoanalysts, in contradiction it seems to the whole of their own doctrine, appear to consider that one of the essential functions of the Ego is the tranquil introjection of the prescriptions and interdictions of the group, without the least bit of personal reflection. This, in my opinion, is more a function of the Superego.

But Harlow, Bowlby, and Zazzo have already described a primary, innate attachment that is not essentially ordered to the satisfactions of other needs such as hunger. Should we look upon this attachment to the mother as a fundamentally different behavior than the exploratory behaviors that succeed it, or as their beginning? As a withdrawal of the infant seeking, like the hermit crab in search of a shell, to retreat to the closeness, protection, and warmth of the womb it has just quitted, or as the dawn of "disinterested" interest for something other, for others, for the whole of reality? Some behavioral psychologists have recently suggested that it is not only a derivative of the desire for the "carrot" or fear of the "stick" which can reward rats for succeeding in problem boxes, but new objects to explore, and Pavlov has said that "the mathematician tends towards truth as the plant towards light." Without doubt it is the same, or partly the same, for the highest rationality of the Ego, for the exercise of our relational thinking, a need that is as imperious and as difficult to repress as other needs.* The satisfaction of this need is accompanied by what the great geologist Pierre Termier called the joy of knowing, and some of the early philosophers happiness, thus distinguishing it from other pleasures without necessarily setting it in opposition to them. *Ama et fac quod vis*: such, according to St. Augustine, is the secret of happiness; it is perhaps not without importance to see more clearly the roots and better understand the mechanisms of what is the most human in man.

Conservations, adjunctions, suppressions, transformations, emergences, and special mechanisms in the progress of consciousness.

Utilitarian concerns, inhibitions, displacements, sublimations, the primor-

---

*"Sie kann damit den entfesselten Erkenntnistrieb nicht mehr hemmen" (F.W. Nietzsche: *Theoretische Studien*).

dial instincts such as hunger, aggression, and sexuality are certainly powerful factors in the progress of consciousness. One of the roots of the desire to know and understand is the will to power. The desire of infants to imitate, equal, and surpass their parents, and not only for genital objectives. The desire of the small child in his immense weakness to become omnipotent: a magician, said one of my young patients, who can annihilate his enemies with one stroke of his magic wand, God Himself...or even more than God! Nevertheless it is probable that the tendency towards consciousness, the movement towards the liberty of universality are, in part, autonomous and innate, i.e., they too are partly instinctual.

Classic psychology has ordered the successive moments of the voluntary, free act as follows: information, deliberation, decision, execution. These days we are more familiar with it and its formerly obscure and hidden antecedents and mechanisms. Some of these mechanisms, without being illogical in the least, differ from a certain normal and conscious adult logic, from, let us say, a certain "sense of simple geometry." I offer some examples: the conflicts between drives, the inhibitions, annulations, combinations, compromises, displacements, sublimations, symbolizations, ritualizations... splitting, projection, introjection, omnipotence, denial, avoidance, repression... the condensation, so striking in dreams, of fragments originating from various sources, united more or less correctly under an apparent unity that satisfies what remains of ordinary waking perception and thought patterns, but which often betray a profound affective tendency, sometimes conscious, sometimes preconscious, and sometimes unconscious. We have already noted some of these special mechanisms. We will get back to them when discussing neuroses, in which they are no longer in touch with the progress of consciousness but with affective fixations, repetitions, and regressions, that go hand in hand with a weakness and narrowness of the Ego.

Degrees of genotype permissiveness in phenotypal realizations.
Two senses of the word "liberty."

The prevailing wisdom has it that innate automatisms result from the realization of genetic virtualities leaning strongly towards a univocal explicitation with little dependence on the characteristics of the actual environment. It is perhaps not paradoxical to affirm the same about our urge to understand the universe, and even, as some among us believe, to sense

God by way of analogy. Perhaps certain of our genetic virtualities themselves are possessed of a strong tendency towards realization in that direction, not only with regard to the formation of *ad hoc* structures but also in respect to our desire and way of making use of these structures, and of playing upon such a marvelous instrument. As for knowing if we are free to make use of them or not, free to play this melody rather than that one and to decide upon the program, if, in sum, we are free to become increasingly free, this is quite another question. It is linked to those dealing with the notion of potentiality, the whole's overwhelming power over the part, the power to say no, the limitation or the absence of limitation by the whole, the diversity and modesty of approaches, the unification or reunification "from above," the unity and diversity... This is not the occasion to enlarge upon these notions. It will be enough to recall than in a Marxist perspective the part's conscious grasp of the totality, man's grasp of the whole of reality, is necessary, although progressive, and the understanding of the profound laws of nature is necessarily overwhelming, which is not the same as saying that it is limiting. Man, so to speak, is subject to necessity under two titles: his genetic code and his milieu, i.e., the Universe, the very same, indeed, that produced the genetic code. Catholics hold to the power of refusal, the power to turn away from the light, along with a corresponding responsibility. Certain Protestants maintain that it is God who decides in advance, at least from our view point: to some He gives necessary and sufficient grace and He refuses it to others. Here I am concerned only with the liberty of universality, whether it does or does not provide man with a power to say no.

CHAPTER IV

Neurotic Obstacles to the Growth of Consciousness and Liberty.

Mechanisms, Diagnostic, Treatment, Prevention of Neuroses.
Some Psychoanalytical Examples of the Meaning and Importance of Conflicts

The obstacles to the development of interior freedom are legion. I here mention but a few. Extreme destitution, hunger, the exhausting labor of workers in former times, as well as subjection of their employers to the imperative of maximizing profits. Consumption elevated to the level of highest duty. Totalitarian societies, with rigid, intolerant dogmas, all manner of inquisitions, restrictions on the freedom of expression and on the duty to inform. Our anxiety in the face of freedom, the "escape from freedom" described by the Austrian psychoanalyst Eric Fromm in 1941: we hardly succeed in casting off old yokes before we find replacements for them;[12] Lorenz echoes this when he speaks of siphoning off *Begeisterung,* or militant enthusiasm, for inhumane ends... Today I will just speak about neurotic obstacles to freedom. The frequency and seriousness of these maladies, the possibility of curing and preventing them, the light they cast on our development, their relationships with many modern problems, such as uncontrolled consumption contrasting with the under-nourishment of the majority of the planet's inhabitants, the abuse of medication and other, less licit drugs, violence of all kinds, disguised or obvious... We do not claim that all these problems are exclusively psychiatric in nature, but they are of interest to the psychiatrist and the psychiatrist has his modest contribution to make.

Neuroses: fixation and repetition diseases.

Under the influence of unfavorable external circumstances, and also of genetic virtualities, affecting either species or only individuals, there is something which initially was not necessarily devoid of adaptability, not without a certain logic and truth, that becomes fixed in the child. This "something" ceases to evolve and yields to forced, automatic, involuntary, unconscious repetitions, which increase in absurdity and inadaptibility as the patient grows older and circumstances and his responsibilities undergo change. The neurotic patient is, if you will, in somewhat the same situation as the instinctual animal when the triggering sign is divorced from the situation in which the reaction originated in the course of the evolution of species: it continues to react in the same way, but henceforth wrongly. He is imprisoned by a sign, by a subjective attitude which no longer has the slightest link with the totality of the present situation. He continues to see reality through his infantile phantasms, in a partial, deformed and stereotyped way, and to react accordingly: the contrary of intelligent and free behavior.

It is somewhat rare to see neurotic repetitions reproduced without modifications, by way of pure and simple identity; this happened in the case of one of my patients, a twenty year old, who spent part of her days and nights repeatedly seeing herself as "a little girl in a short dress, holding the hand of her mama." Her mother died suddenly when she was eight years old, and immediately thereafter she was placed in an orphanage.

Most frequently the repetition is "analogical." The subsequent situations and reactions at one and the same time contain elements identical to those which contained the initial situations and reactions, as well as different ones. Through the distance of time and repression these differences increasingly disguise the basic identity from the patient, preventing, as they say, the dawning of awareness. The pursuit of the identity beneath the difference, i.e., of the analogy or resemblance that expresses the fixation and repetition, is the constant concern of the psychoanalyst. He comes to think analogically, symbolically, like his patients. Like them he is a "structuralist," but he is an aware one. Initially, they are not.

Even though neuroses are fundamentally illnesses of arrest and repetition, they are not necessarily devoid of all spontaneous evolution. At first the language used to express the same problems changes with age: for example, the successive modes of expression of aggression and combat, the oral, anal, urethral, phallic, and genital. Furthermore, real or imagined experiences lived out at different periods and at different points of development can make one with the primitive, repressed nucleus to the extent they correspond to it and are both drawn by it and rejected from the field of conscious and pre-conscious representations. Freud called this secondary repression. One particularly interesting composition or condensation is that of pre- or extra-genital combat with the Oedipal attitude; Othello will furnish us with a remarkable example of this. Finally, certain defensive or partially defensive processes, some early, such as splitting and projection, some a little later, like obsessional ritualization, can come to cast over neuroses an appearance of evolution.

Jackson's theory of neuroses.

The theory of neuroses is easily inserted into the broad theory of pathological automatisms constructed during the 19th century by the English neurologist Jackson, principally based upon his experience with epilepsies and later extended to other domains of neurology and psychiatry.[13]

For Jackson the path of evolution proceeds from the more simple to the more complex, from the more organized to the less organized, from the less voluntary to the more voluntary; organized is taken by Jackson in the sense of rigid organization; the law of "complexity-consciousness" of the anthropologist and prehistorian Teilhard de Chardin echoes Jackson's law of evolution a century later.

The pathological dissolution of a higher and subsequent level that had assumed control (particularly an *inhibiting* control) of lower and prior automatisms effects their release. This is readily evident in senile dementia. In the case of neuroses it is not so much the dissolution of the Ego as its weakness, its failure to grow, which are correlative with the invasion of consciousness and behavior by neurotic automatisms. Or, if you prefer, there are the fixations, the developmental arrests, that exhibit their force and persistence. An analogous remark applies perhaps equally to the eventual direct excitation of epileptic *patterns*, which lead to some minor reservations, corrections, or precisions for Jackson's theory in the light of current data in neurology and psychiatry.

Now let us compare a temporal epileptic automatism and a neurotic one: the woman who repeatedly kept seeing herself during epileptic seizures as a young factory worker of thirteen years, dressed in a plaid apron, and the neurotic patient who was held prey by that constant recall of the image of herself at eight, a little girl holding the hand of her mother who was to die a short time later. The close similarity of their symptoms is obvious, notably their automatic, forced, rigid, repetitive, and obscuring character: at one and the same time the patient is unable to prevent the repetition and while it is taking place he perceives nothing else. The resemblance is underscored still more by the existence of mixed cases in which the patient is suffering from both a neurosis and a temporal epilepsy, with the same stereotyped pattern being played out now during an epileptic seizure, now as neurotic. It is not without interest to note that Shakespeare made Othello, who in our opinion was fundamentally neurotic, a victim of epileptic seizures. Whatever, along side the resemblances there are considerable differences between epilepsy and neuroses, first of all in the matter of their respective ways of formation and treatment.

Neuroses caused by Oedipal fixations. Neuroses caused by pre-Oedipal fixations, sometimes called "psychoses."

The first of these consists of persisting Oedipal, genital, and "triangular" attitudes, which begin to appear normally between ages one and three, but which usually start to fade during subsequent years. This is the forbidden genital desire of the child for its parents, principally for the one of the opposite sex. The second are linked more to aggression and combat, to what Freud towards the end of his life called the "death wish." These have been particularly studied by one part of post-Freudian psychoanalysis, notably the school of Melanie Klein.[14, 15] They are explained as the result of conflict fixations that developed before the genital phase, and sometimes called "psychoses," the advantage of so distinguishing them from Oedipal neuroses being, according to many psychiatrists, strongly counterbalanced by the possibility of confusion with other mental illnesses. I want to focus briefly on this second type of neuroses. It seems to me they are less known than the first.

Dependence, attachment, love, and hate
in the first relationships between mother and child.

There are not only dependency, attachment and love in this symbiotic relationship between mother and child, in this kind of bipolar unity that Spitz calls a "dyade." The relationship includes elements of aggression, hate, and fear as well.

Whether caused by dependence, a real or imaginary frustration, suffering, discomfort, or whatever, grimaces, screams, and rages are frequent in the infant. Analogy also leads us to suppose that it can experience anguish and fear, principally, we are often told by child psychoanalysts, through the unconscious projection of its own anger and destructive tendencies onto its mother, as well as through fear of retaliation. This perhaps ignores somewhat the lessons of ethology about intra-specific aggression and its weak or non-existent inhibition among men, the frequency and intensity with which a mother both desires and dreads the killing of her own children, the "Abraham complex..." It bears repeating that along with subjective distortions the child can have perfectly good reasons to be afraid, even of its own parents, its own mother. This is all super-added to the birth trauma, to having been violently ejected through a narrow tunnel into a different, outside world, hostile, in a way, despite the most attentive and enlightened care of midwives and obstetricians. The rage itself, the convulsion and suffocation that follow, can be resented by the infant as a new suffering and a new danger.

The split between love and hate. Imaginary projected adjunctions.

If it is certain that the young infant manifests sketches of transitional mimicry, some conflicts and composition-reactions—perhaps not so apparent in Klein's psychoanalysis—it is no less true that at that age expressions of beatific satisfaction and manifestations of rage or despair are often "total" and lacking in nuance.

Melanie Klein has called this splitting between hate and love "schizophrenia." Though etymologically exact, like the word "psychosis" it runs the risk of confusion with different mental illnesses which others call by the same name. Furthermore, we do not think it evident, at least at the outset, that this splitting would be a defensive reaction, as Kleinian psychoanalysts claim in the wake of Freud. Initially it is probably the sign, the behavioral aspect of an insufficient cerebral development rather than a "defensive projection outside of the death wish." Let us recall the findings of clinical anatomy, the fact that for the young infant reactions to innate signs dominate, along with analysis without true synthesis and understanding of the whole, as with instinctual animals.

A little later, with cerebral maturation and first experiences, it is probable that the splitting also takes on a defensive aspect, which increases, prolongs, or even fixates the splitting, a defense against ambiguity and the anguish that it provokes: it is easier to love totally that which is totally good and to detest totally that which is totally bad than to fine tune one's feelings according to the nuances of reality; it also provides protection, preservation, and the maintaining at one's disposal of "good objects" isolated and protected against destructive tendencies... At the same time the splitting focuses increasingly upon unreal objects, notably as a result of the unconscious processes of projection and deflection which bestow all the subject's capacity for love upon the good object and all its hate, destructivity, and fear upon the evil one... Thus to the "sin of omission" deriving from an excessive analysis, a lack of synthesis and understanding of the whole, there is added another kind of subjective distortion. To aspects of reality that are really good or evil there correspond two doubly subjective worlds: one totally good, the other totally evil. Both derive from imaginary splitting and additions.

Some examples of neuroses with emphasis on splitting, projection, etc.

Under certain conditions, in certain persons, we observe an exacerbation, a prolongation, and even a fixation of the processes of splitting, projection, etc.; then instead of forming the beginning and basis of a normal development, these latter give rise to exceptionally serious neuroses. I offer a few examples.

One of my young patients, eight years old, has a mother who herself is ill. She is subject to sudden, unexpected emotional changes; without any transition or apparent motive she can make sudden swings between the most tender love and fits of anger as sudden as they are fierce. On more than one occasion I myself felt a little uneasy! The child is in a continual fight with his parents, his brother, and his companions. His interior world is a place of "parental imagos," at once split, exaggerated, displaced, and marked by substitutions: thieving brigands who torture children set against good policemen, gigantic and horrible animals, "a diplodocus as big as a house" capable of reducing him to mush, against whom he is defended by other animals, good and powerful lions and gorillas, his protectors and friends. The projection is obvious in the transference: after having spent a session biting my cushion in a rage, watching me with hatred all the while, he drew a picture of me as an ogre ready to devour him. In the evening, with his little brother, he liked to play a game about ogres and sandwiches; they would be two slices of ham in an eider-down quilt sandwich waiting in terror for the ogres to come from their parents' room and devour them. Oral destructivity is partly more conscious in the mixed phantasy in which he is a little fly eaten by the diplodocus but too small for the latter to do him any harm, and then he in turn devouring it from inside. This is the child who, when other means of attack and defense proved insufficient, transformed himself into an all-powerful magician, or God, even "more than God..." Among other ways the introjection, together with the projection, is marked by the "interior" character of the phantasies. The interpretation takes on added precision when we note that his father is a policeman and that there are frequent marital quarrels. The awakening happened in the transference and I gave the parents some pieces of advice. The child then left in his third year of treatment, somewhat prematurely but well on his way to good health. It is possible that he will need a little additional work at a later date.

I had another patient, a young psychology student, who since adolescence had been terrified by the idea of seeing her father turn into a wolf and break into her room in that form at night. You will note the mixed character of the image, at once oral, fecal, and phallic, which is both desired and feared. In her first transference dream immediately following our first session she found herself in a room resembling mine, with a large white dog behind her. As a matter of fact, during the initial months on my couch she manifested an attitude of both aggression and terror, aggravated by the lack of visual control in the psychoanalytical position.

A young obese woman of thirty, who had kept to her room for a number of years, had had several sojourns in psychiatric clinics. Aside from that she was charming and, in a way, showed a very active intelligence. Her mother recalls that she had been an extremely voracious baby, and that she had been suckled until the age of eighteen months, when she was weaned abruptly in a manner that apparently is still used in the Italian countryside. The breast was offered one last time, smeared with soot!

She recalls nothing else out of the ordinary about her child's reactions, except for a brief period in which she tearfully refused food. Other frustrations were subsequently added to the first. The more conscious of them were the bankruptcy of her father, abandoning the family home for a poor house, and the need to give up the studies she had her heart set on and learn accounting, which she detested, in order to help her father. Her own subjective attitudes most likely led her to leave the young men whom she liked and so added to her frustration, despair, anger, fear... For this young woman the world was split into two parts, divided, as Othello says, "by all the height that separates Heaven from Hell."

Hell, for example, are her reveries of a horrible country of anthropaphagic debauches where "Turks," children, and miscarried fetuses are tortured and chopped up to make sausages, or cooked in soups of urine and fecal matter. Heaven are the dreams she had in which she was called by a God of goodness to live eternally in a marvelous land with the grandfather she once adored, now restored to life. You will note the projection and introjection of numerous kinds of sadistic phantasies: oral, urethral, fecal, of mincing and aggression involving the contents of the maternal womb in the first instance, and a touch of the Oedipal in the second. The latter (unless a split has occured) is accentuated, once the tunnel on the way to the "heavenly Jerusalem" is traversed, by an immense, magnificent, but perfidious and dangerous *sea* (in French "*mer*"—sea—suggests "*mère*"—mother). I would like to add that the "simple" form of the Oedipal reaction is never complicated by such a split between love and hate, nor embellished with such vibrant and such archaic forms of sadism. The psychoanalysis was interrupted shortly after it had begun, under the pretext of financial reasons. The real reasons were twofold. On the one hand was her fear of the psychoanalyst and on the other her fear of losing the "secondary benefits" of her illness: she faced the prospect of ending her self isolation and having to work in this terrible world. I had been subjected to a rapid "abreaction," i.e. a critical transfer, a repetition in the course of which I was resented as the greatest of her persecutors. She went so far as to see in a dream my couch draped in black upon which was placed a coffin that contained the remains of patients I had tortured and murdered.

I would add that in the case of the former patient, the young psychologist, along side an unconscious deflection and projection, the death wishes against others and even her own son were partly conscious, and in that sense they were somewhat less serious. What prompted her consulting me, her request for treatment and her perseverance in the same, was the spiteful feelings she experienced towards her husband and son.

Progress towards synthesizing and the grasp of the whole, decrease in imaginary adjunctions during childhood development.
Perspectives of M. Klein, R. Spitz, and J. Piaget.
The "depressive position" of psychoanalysts following Klein.
Chronological shifts.

The first days, weeks, or months of the child's development are characterized by a dominance of analysis and a relative lack of synthesis. There is little understanding of the whole. The principal causes are doubtless the brain's immaturity and the predominance of innate reactions to signs that are somehow isolated from their context, and which are prolonged by early conditioning, which is itself related to a somewhat diffuse spectrum of signs. Joy and rage often manifest themselves in the raw, out of context, and completely devoid of nuance. A series of strongly grounded indirect arguments, of "reconstructions" and analogical extrapolations leading back to origins, suggests to the psychoanalyst that fears of vengeance and unconscious projection over-layer real motives of love and hate (the latter perhaps somewhat underestimated). The unconscious projections combine with the goodness and evil of initially split objects, and transforms them into partly subjective "imagos" that are all the more cleaved.

But already there is a certain proportion between the gesture response and stimulations of different intensities, a certain "mosaic synthesis" of "the great parliament of the instincts," i.e., of many different kinds of innate behaviors, an initial connection between initial conditionings and experiences, all of which constitutes, as it were, the first indications of future progress. As the mind and organic structure together mature in general, along with experience and learning in the face of reality, or at least in confrontation with serious interior or exterior obstacles, there soon follows a diminution of the splitting and the projections, and an advancement in synthetic, or, more exactly, analytic-synthetic thought. Little by little the child becomes capable of synthesizing the agreeable and disagreeable aspects of its mother, then of the world, to mingle with ever increasing nuance its own affects of love and aggression and then to replace and sublimate them. At the same time the old images little by little lose their force, and the old subjective distortions lessen. This results in an increasingly true perspective on things and progress in ability to understand the whole, which are the first steps towards the liberty of universality.

It also results in the advent of guilt and of the desire to make reparation when the aggression and destructivity bear upon an object or person known at the time, or remembered shortly afterwards, to have another side as well, one of goodness, helpfulness, generosity, and worthy of love. This is what psychoanalysts in the tradition of Klein term the "depressive position," modeled after the "schizo-paranoid" just described, and similarly a subsequent base for further progress or for neurotic fixations, depending upon circumstances and constitutions.

Spitz' well known sequence describes the progressive synthesis which the child makes of aspects, especially visual ones, of its mother, a synthesis marked by changes in what sets off a smile or mimicry of anxiety.[16] Visual pursuit, at first triggered by anything that is shiny and moves, rapidly, and with clear preference, comes to be set off by the eyes of the observer. Smiling, at first a simple indication of having one's fill, or observed during drowsiness with no apparent reason, soon comes to be triggered by the sight of the upper part of any human face, and even a proffered face mask. According to Spitz, the infant would not recognize the personal visage of its mother until about eight months, and thus not until then would it smile at her preferentially. He even felt (and many authors have some doubts on this point) that, from that point on, the infant would systematically exhibit fear at the visage of a stranger. Let us note that, according Melanie Klein, the synthesis of the mother's affective aspects would begin earlier, with the end of the first trimester.

This is not the place to give a detailed description of, or even to summarize, the extensive and marvelous contributions of the school of Piaget to the field of genetic epistemology. They deal more with intellectual than affective development. One fundamental sequence of it, which has a direct correlation with synthesis, is the progressive recognition of the permanence of the object, along with its various qualities, such as form, volume, weight, etc.[17] To the shifts in the knowledge of various permanencies, as observed by Piaget, we may add the astonishing retardation, or even the impossibility, of affectively synthesizing the object in the case of certain neurotics. It is always amazing to see that an otherwise intelligent adult, who has long since been able to grasp the

corporal permanence of the object in question, behaves affectively as if
he had two alternative objects before him, the one worthy of his
unbounded hate, the other of all his love.

The mix of stages in neuroses. Neuroses with both pre-Oedipal and Oedipal characters. The Othello complex.

As long as it persists, the great pre-Oedipal split, with its retinue of other
archaic mechanisms such as projection, unconscious deflection of the
death instinct and of childish love, whether pre- or extra-genital, accentu-
ates and modifies the rivalries, interdictions, inferiorities, jealousies,
rages, and fears in the triangular relationship. This relationship is still
more complicated when both the sexual rival as well as the object of the
child's incestuous desire, either by substitution, displacement, or directly,
arise out of the split maternal imago, or, to put it better, the two separate
maternal imagos...the good mother and the bad mother of times past. As
for any remnants of the "depressed state," these increase guilt and the
desire to make reparation.

I will defer comment about Chessex's *L'Ogre,* since I have read only
its critique. But if what the latter says is true, namely that Chessex sees
his father in the ogre, the character of this phantasm, at once split, exaggerated (and therefore likely to be partly projective) and fundamentally
oral-sadistic, strongly suggests that it is probably no more than a displacement of a split mother imago which contains mainly the destructive tendencies of ... Chessex himself as a child. Note, however, that the figure of
the ogre can likewise suggest castration...

The combination of the two stages is a classic cause of genital sadism,
the primitive, sado-masochistic symbiotic relation being nuanced by a
genital touch as the child grows. The story of this evolution, this addition
or compositing let us say, was easy to follow in one of my most severely
ill patients. A twenty-six year old male, married, the father of a family,
had killed (in his imagination) some thousands, or tens of thousands of
women since the tender years of his infancy, and always in the same way.
He plunged a knife into their hearts and then masturbated at the sight of
their agony. In the analysis everything indicated that we were dealing
with a condensed, partially substituted, displaced, and transformed image
of an attack against the mother's breast and a violent sexual penetration of

her. Less frequently he used to imagine, with equal pleasure, that he was undergoing the same fate at the hands of a man. Now and again, for a long period of time, a vague, indefinable image arose, filled with a series of contrary emotions: a blank, uniform surface suddenly troubled and stirred by waves. I would hesitate to assert that we were dealing with a remembrance of the breasts' cleavage. The analysis ended a little prematurely, towards the beginning of the fourth year, shortly after a transference dream and an unfortunate coincidence: in his dream he saw himself near the hen-house where, as a small child, he from time to time used to sacrifice a chicken and then bury it while singing church hymns. I was chasing him, endowed with super-human strength, trying to put him into the "Sleep-Machine," a condensed memory, redolent of death and castration, of an operation for phimosis which was unfortunately performed at that time. A few days later he had met an ambulance and two hospital attendants in front of my house, who had been called to bring to the hospital an older neighbor of mine who had just suffered an attack. Shortly thereafter he wrote to tell me he was going to continue his psychoanalysis with one of my psychologist colleagues.

In the case of a mixed neurosis we often see a genital frustration, real in the case of the child, frequently imaginary in the case of the Oedipal adult, trigger, like any frustration, a regression towards the great pre-Oedipal, pre- or extra-genital split.

Othello provides us with the drama of frustration, envy, jealousy, "the green eyed monster that feeds upon itself." It is also the drama of splitting, exacerbated and maintained through projection, which permits the most total love and insane adoration to be replaced by senseless hate and murder. Though Othello is the protagonist, Shakespeare also makes use of other personages, other characters, in order to cast light upon the complexity of the problem.

Iago is motivated by racial hatred, by the jealousy of an inferior towards a superior, by despair at seeing Othello prefer young Cassio, who has only "bookish theory," to himself, who has demonstrated his value on the field of battle. Before adopting Othello as his nephew-in-law, Brabantio hates him for his color and for taking from him the niece whom he loves. Iago whispers in his ear that an "old black ram is tupping your white ewe." Cassio, "good Michael," has little tolerance for alcohol and, after imbibing, kills one of his best friends for an insignificant offense. Emilia, Iago's wife, is furious at the dependent lot of women. Full of hatred, Iago, who

accuses Othello of all the sins in the world, reproaches him also, inciden-
tally and without much conviction, of having bedded Emilia.

In the character of Othello, Oedipal traits mingle with pre-Oedipal,
Oedipus with Orestes, and probably also with a trace of Abraham and
Jocasta: Desdemona, indeed, is much younger than Othello. She is young
enough to be his daughter. Othello is a strong, proud fighting man hungry
for power and glory. It is with the story of his exploits and victories that
he has won Desdemona. But he is frustrated by his race, which the Vene-
tians basically despise; Desdemona herself feels obliged to declare that
she has seen "the true face of Othello in his soul"! He must declare that he
is a "son of a king." Othello's relationship with Desdemona is one of
extreme dependence; for him she is "the pure source of his life"...and
therefore on the verge of being over-whelming: for love of her, he
laments, he must renounce his aspirations, "the treasures of the sea," symbols of freedom, travel, and adventure... Psychoanalysts would say that
the relation is hardly less symbiotic than that between the infant and its
mother. Othello shifts easily from one extreme to the other. His life is like
a small boat cast upon a wild sea, tossed about at the whim of gigantic billows as high and as low as "the distance between heaven and hell." A few
words from Iago and the pure source of his life becomes "a cistern for
foul toads to knot and gender in." His fury and his vengeance bear not
upon his imaginary rival—he charges Iago to dispose of him as an
afterthought—but upon his wife, an imaginary substitute for a split maternal imago. His illusion that she is totally frustrating, dangerous, and hateful, follows quick upon the opposite illusion that she was totally good.
Murder succeeds adoration, and in turn yields place to the despair of
abandonment and of loss, equal at least to moral guilt. Othello takes his
own life.

Let us take it a step further. Iago, the devilish instigator, ends up taking
complete possession of the noble Othello by substituting his own dark,
obscure soul for the latter's once luminous soul. We have strong reasons to
think that it is the split within the ego, Othello's "schizophrenia," that
Shakespeare intended to symbolize. He paints him as ill, an "epileptic."
Two centuries after Shakespeare, a little before Freud, one century before
the Mason affair, the "Jesus-Satan" of California and the drugs that release
the drunken Furies, *Doctor Jekyll and Mister Hyde* echoed the Othello-
Iago theme upon the stage in other settings and ways of symbolization.

Re-examination of the various sources of normal development. The causes of neurotic fixation. Persistence of innate or learned behaviors, whether normal or pathological, which are not typically neurotic.

Among the factors in the growth of consciousness and freedom, to the "utilitarianism" of reason, the sublimation of such instincts as self-preservation, self-satisfaction, aggression and sexuality, and probably other instincts like that of service, there is most likely added another innate tendency that is no less instinctual or powerful: the quest for contact, for relationship, exploration, and the conscious grasp of reality. We have glimpsed all the complexity of this dialectic in normal development, as well as in neurotic fixations, repetitions, and regressions.

It seems to us that there are a number of causes for neurotically arrested development: specific heredity, individual heredity or constitutional typology, a certain voracity, a certain force, a certain obstinacy, a certain inability to endure frustration, perhaps more hereditary than learned. There are also errors in education, inadequacies within the environment, particularly in early infancy, catastrophic events such as war, certain particularities in the social system, the vagaries of life, chance encounters, etc.

More difficult is the question of the eventual persistence, either normal or pathological, of certain innate behaviors, of certain acquired habits other than neurotic. Think, for example, of certain total reactions to isolated signs, completely without reflection, adapted or absurd, where it is hard to say whether we are dealing with residues of innate reactions, good or bad habits, or neurotic traits. Consider those "constitutional psychopathies" that earlier psychiatrists made so much of, and most particularly Professor Ferdinand Morel, one of my mentors... This is not the place to pursue them, but still it is necessary to point out their possible existence.

The psychoanalytical treatment of neuroses. The use of palliative medicaments. Prophylaxis.

I will not dwell at length on the psychoanalytical treatment of neuroses, which is well known. It aims to attenuate or to suppress definitively pathological automatisms of the mind through increased awareness, and particularly by means of a privileged human relationship, the relation between the therapist and the patient, a lived, affective relation, filled at first with unconscious "transferred" pathological repetitions that are progressively explained to the patient and progressively normalized.

In our opinion the therapeutic use of medicaments in serious neuroses is indicated only when psychoanalytical treatment is impossible, whether because of the patient's financial or social situation, or because of a character inadequacy in the patient or his family, or because the patient is too old. We feel that medicaments are palliative rather than capable of resolving anything radically. We are not opposed to administering medicaments *a minima* during the analytical cure, for a limited time and in a measure that does not mask the symptomology and, most notably, does not hinder the transference and the profound, durable transformation of the therapeutic human relationship. On the contrary, they can be very useful and in a certain way sufficient in "reactive states," or for purposes of adapting, deconditioning, reconditioning, and changing habits in mild cases or cases other than neurotic. We are quick to give a few vitamins, a few minerals, some magnesium, to those of our patients who suffer from spasmophilia along with their neurosis. Depending on the case, other psychotherapeutic methods can be utilized.*

Prophylaxis consists in treating the neuroses of parents, counsel about education, social hygiene, and, generally, in the amelioration or the transformation of social and socio-cultural conditions.

Meaning and the importance of conflicts in the progress, stagnation, or regression of consciousness and freedom. Some examples from psychoanalysis.

There is no question here of what philosophers, theologians, and even advanced physicists would call the supreme contradiction, that of "creation *ex nihilo*" or total destruction, *ad nihilum,* but only of lesser ones, at least by comparison.

We have seen the positive, constructive, creative or "co-creative" character of conflicts in Darwin's theory, as well as the successful results of conflicting reactions generating changes in objectives and goals, in sublimations, which ethologists, psychologists, and psychoanalysts have observed. We could give many other examples. We also know that under other circumstances the same conflicts, or analogous ones, can be the cause of stagnation, regression, or premature, inadequate, useless, destruction.

---

*See "The goals, methods, and limits of psychotherapy" in the present work.

To hold ourselves to two psychoanalytical examples, let us recall how a successfully managed and well resolved Oedipal conflict contributes to adult formation through emulation, identification, the desire to equal or surpass, the changing of object, of goal even, the sublimation. And conversely, how that same conflict, badly managed and poorly resolved, can cause damage, the same as victories too easily come by, and too incomplete, due to the physical or moral absence of the sex rival, or the overly seductive, possessive, or permissive attitude of the parental object of incestuous desire. Let us also recall how important is the contribution of pre- or extra-genital conflicts, likewise well or badly handled or resolved, in a familial, social context adequate or inadequate for the formation of, to put it a little stylistically, heros and saints, or murderers, or simply well or poorly adjusted people.

One final word about Freud's "death instinct." Is it simply a matter, as Lorenz thinks, of intra-specific aggressiveness and its derivatives, by displacements, sublimations, and goal changes, even directed against the self? Was this all there was, joined to the sex instinct, in the case of that patient who could delight in the phantasy of his own murder, his own agony, like that of the women he used to kill in his imagination? Another of my patients, a "persecuted-persecutor" who dreamed of nothing but wounds and bruises, recalled a fit of rage as a child, during which his wanting to strangle his mother ended up in an attempt at self strangulation... Is there not already in the very young infant a kind of obscure presentiment of how fragile and brief is life, of how real and immense are its dangers both from within and without, of how inescapable is death, of the possible consequences of unsatisfied hunger, of a rage pushed to the point of suffocation, of a homicidal gesture on the part of its mother, of a difficult birth? Despair, the feeling that life is not worth living, are they not sometimes founded on solid grounds, as well as or more so than a morbid disproportion, a gulf never filled between what one gets and what one wants? The "sad Sundays" of Hitler's Germany before the war, were they not really as somber as death? Is not the instinct towards service, like the sexual instinct in Freud's first topic, in a way opposed, sometimes radically, to that of self-preservation? Natural selection, dedifferentiation, the place left to youth, are they not fundamental components of life? Does not the building of new molecules utilize the elements of the old ones and therefore require a certain destruction of the latter? As well as conservation and composition, does not emergence demand a certain suppression? What did Freud really mean by THANATOS? Why and in what sense did he oppose it to EROS?

CHAPTER V

Summary

I have spoken of some of the neurotic obstacles to man's (and woman's) blossoming, and of the way a psychoanalytic cure, i.e., the dawning of awareness and the modification through transference, can reduce or suppress these repetitive, unconscious, involuntary, coercive, limiting automatisms—the contrary of free behavior—which result from the unhappy conjunction of an inadequate environment during childhood and from certain hereditary predispositions, particularly that of having a total reaction to signs isolated from context.

I explained how the "Othello complex," without a doubt more primitive and more basic than the Oedipus complex, arises from special relationships between the very young child and its mother at the time of the "dyadic symbiosis," exhibiting an exaggerated and above all abnormally persisting split between love and hate. This pre-Oedipal, fixated split overflows, under-girds, and nuances the genital problems that come later; in the case of Othello it turns the man's fury and vengeance against not the rival but the woman, an imaginary substitute for a split maternal imago, an illusion seen now as totally good, now as totally frustrating, dangerous, and hateful. The murder succeeds adoration and gives place to despair.

I have tried to show in what way the understanding of neurotic mechanisms contributes, just as it does to prevention or treatment, to that of normal development, the growth within us of the faculty of perceiving the whole, of locating parts in their relationships with each other and with the whole, that interior freedom which penetrates, humanizes, and increases our more humble joys. As to conflicts studied by psychoanalysts, I recalled that the better as well as the worse can arise out of struggle.

BIBLIOGRAPHY

1. André-Thomas, Y. Chesni, S. Saint-Anne Dargassies: *The Neurological Examination of the Infant*. Translated from the French and with a preface by R. C. MacKeith, P. E. Polani, E. Clayton-Jones, National Spastics Society & Heinemann, London, 1960. Out of print.

2. Y. Chesni: "Sur le cri et quelques autres comportements mimiques innés examinés pendant les premiers jours de la vie," Revue de Laryngologie, *91*, 5–6, 1970, 339–357, Portmann, Bordeaux.

3. A. Minkowski: *Regional Development of the Brain in Early Life*. Blackwell, Oxford, Edinburgh, 1967.

4. K. Lorenz, *On Aggression*. Translated by M. K. Wilson, Harcourt-Brace, San Diego, 1974.

5. D. Anzieu, J. Bowlby, R. Chauvin, F. Duyckaerts, H. M. F. Harlow, C. Koupernik, S. Lebovici, K. Lorenz, Ph. Malrieu, R. A. Spitz, D. Widlocher, R. Zazzo: *L'attachement*. Delachaux & Niestlé, Neuchâtel, 1974.

6. F. Jacob: *The Logic of Life. A History of Heredity*. Pantheon, New York, 1982.

7. J. Monod: *Chance and Necessity*. Random House, New York, 1972.

8. W. Penfield, H. Jasper: *Epilepsy and the Functional Anatomy of the Human Brain*. Little, Brown & Company, Boston, 1954.

9. Y. Chesni: *Dialectical Realism. Towards a Philosophy of Growth*. Translated from the French by J. P. Zenk, The Live Oak Press, Palo Alto, 1987.

10. Y. Chesni: "The goals, methods, and limits of psychotherapy," in the present work.

11. S. Freud: *Outline of Psychoanalysis*. Edited and translated from the German by J. Strachey, Norton, New York, 1970.

12. E. Fromm: *Escape from Freedom*. Avon, The Hearst Corporation, New York, 1965.

13. Y. Chesni: "Petite contribution au centenaire de la théorie de Jackson," Revue d'Oto-Neuro-Ophthalmologie, *XLII*, 7, 1970, 416–422.

14. H. Segal: *Introduction to the Work of Melanie Klein*. The Hogarth Press and the Institute of Psychoanalysis, London, 1973.

15. M. Klein, P. Heimann, S. Isaacs, J. Riviere: *Developments in Psychoanalysis*. De Capo, Jersey City, 1982.

16. R. Spitz: *The First Year of Life: A Psychoanalytic Study of Normal and Deviant Development of Object Relations*. International Universities Press, Madison, Ct., 1966.

17. T. Gouin-Décarie: *Intelligence et affectivité chez le jeune enfant. Etude expérimentale de la notion d'objet chez Jean Piaget et de la relation objectale*. Delachaux & Niestlé, Neuchâtel, 1973.

PART THREE

A Tentative Interpretation of St. John of the Cross Within Natural, Open Perspectives*

* Conference given November 29, 1978, at the
Cercle d'Etudes Philosophiques d'Annecy
(Conférences et Débats, *4,* 1978 and *3,* 1979).

For the most part, on a sufficiently large scale, the evolution of living beings reveals a progressive increase in independence in respect to signs out of context, in the ability to locate parts in respect to each other and the whole; among men we observe a divergence of opinion regarding the meaning of the "All" and the place of human existence. These are simply realities of natural history. Such are the biological and spiritual backgounds we must outline prior to our effort in understanding the meaning of St. John of the Cross and his "Ascent of Mount Carmel."

CHAPTER VI

Biological Background

The evolution of energy, radiation, matter, and life.

About ten billion years ago, physicists tell us,[1] an "infinitely" heated and condensed point or core unit exploded, begetting our expanding and cooling universe. Seven hundred thousand years later, the universe was sufficiently cooled, matter came to prevail over radiation, elementary particles condensed into nuclei, electrons and nuclei formed stable atoms, galaxies and stars began to take shape. About what happened before, the distant future, the far distances of space within the present, the why, the "why this and not that" we know nothing, neither do we know whether we can know, nor even if these words make any sense. Though cosmology is growing more precise, the domain of faith, and philosophy as well, remains vast. Let us proceed on the subject of "how."

   In the beginning simple, light atoms predominate: hydrogen, a little helium. Time goes on, the elementary particles condense, increasingly heavier and increasingly complex atoms make their appearance. A little more time passes and the atoms combine among themselves, forming molecules. Four or five billion years ago our planet begins to exist, the cooling continues, and the molecules become more and more complex. Three or three and a half billion years ago life appeared on earth, with its simple alphabet of five bases and twenty amino acids, and its triple characteristic of reproduction, variation, and the selection of favorable variations, stockpiling more and more information, with a negative entropy running counter to the presumed increase in universal entropy. With intramolecular liaisons using much less energy than intranuclear liaisons, matter becomes more pliable. As syntheses become increasingly complex and diverse, and with the increase in the need both to destroy and conserve the old in order to build the new, the great laws of *correlation, differentiation, conservation, suppression,* and *emergence* continue to manifest themselves. Despite all our own originality, we are composed of primordial elements and still contain genetic programs that mark the beginnings of life. In another way, that of science, we rejoin the perspective of the ancient Upanishads: "You are that, unity within diversity, oneness with the totality..."[2]

Progress in the liberty of universality.

Let us direct our time exploring machine towards this last period and set it on increased enlargement. The development of life—covering three and a half billion years—is represented by one meter. In the last millimeter, three and a half million years ago, our direct ancestors appeared, hominoids possessing a brain more developed than that of other animals, fangless, walking upright, their hands grasping weapons, continuing like many of their lesser brothers to engage in mutual combat, yet assisting each other in the hunt, the defense of their territory, the protection of home, society, and homeland, for the feeding, protection, and upbringing of their children....[3]

Viewed on this scale of time, the evolution of living beings shows, with absolutely no ambiguity, a progressive increase of independence in respect to signs isolated from context, of the ability to situate parts in respect to the whole. This is what I have called the *tendency towards the liberty of universality.*[4]

The male robin, at mating time, furiously attacks other male robins. The reaction is quite admirable, promoting victory, the reproduction and transmission of the most suitable hereditary qualities,[5] an adaptation scarcely affected, and then only occasionally and for brief periods of time, by aberrant sexual selection and tastes. But the obverse of the adaptation and the unconscious logic of instinct, the genetic fruit of past selective confrontations, is the stupidity of the animal that does not understand what it does. With exactly the same fury it attacks a stuffed robin, or any bit of red material. It is prisoner to a sign, blinded by a sign. It has no grasp of context. Similarly the goose bestows its maternal love upon stones equipped with a peeping microphone and kills its own young if it becomes deaf.[6] The newborn human baby pursues with its lips, tongue, and head whatever object tickles its labial commisure, be it as uneatable as the observer's finger.[7]

In contrast with these innate, ultra-analytical reactions, lacking synthesis and in a way unconscious, intelligence increases, not negating but integrating, prolonging, and exceeding them. Man becomes capable of understanding the world and himself as well, of acting more freely, indeed, as believers affirm, of becoming conscious of God, or at least beginning to do so. However, according to the mystics and various philosophers,[8, 9] intelligence in its own turn must yield to different and higher forms of consciousness, relationships, and ways of existence. A little like how discursive explanation adds to the enjoyment of music but remains insufficient. Charity, St. Paul reminds us, is the greatest of the virtues, and without it the others amount to nothing. And, as St. John of the Cross advises us, "If you stop at some one thing, you do not cast yourself upon the All." But opinions vary in respect to the nature of the All, and the possibility of knowing the All—which means something quite other than knowing everything…

Progress of the analytic-synthetic dialectic. Its relationships with the dialectic of conflict.

With varying degrees of perspecuity, through different approaches, and under different aspects, modern naturalists perceive, describe, and try to explain this tendency of life towards ever greater liberty. Inspired by Spencer, Jackson sees the evolution of individuals, as well as that of species, proceeding from the more simple to the more complex, from the more organized (i.e., the more rigidly organized) to the less organized, from the more automatic to the more voluntary.[10] Teilhard de Chardin echoes this notion with his law of complexity-consciousness, perhaps better called the law of differentiation-correlation-consciousness,[11] which in no way contradicts the simplifying, purgative, and unitive experiences with which we will be dealing. Pavlov, with the signs of signs and the second system of signalization, the verbal sign "capable of abstraction and generalization," sees "the mathematician tending towards truth as a plant inclines towards light."[12] Describing the evolution of intelligence, Piaget stresses the interiorization and reversibility of operations as conditions of their greater generalization. Freud, somewhat the utilitarian, places the intelligent Ego at the service of satisfying the primordial instincts in ways that are most adapted and which involve the least danger from society. Like the Buddha, he explains what he calls the religious illusion as the projection onto Heaven of our unsatisfied desires, and among them he gives chief place to our desire for an all powerful Father who begets us, loves us, watches over, guides, and accords us what we ask of Him.[13] He perceives less clearly that instinct towards disinterested interest, probably autonomous in part, in beings and in Being,[14] which can go as far as desiring to see, understand, and love the "All" and, a fact that is as indubitable as it is extraordinary, wanting in some way or another to transform ourselves into the "All" and become like it.

Life obviously offers us other forms of movement, differing forms, whether opposed or contrary: stagnation, regression—beginning with weakness, vulnerability, senility, death, the ephemeral nature of individuals. But in a certain way, viewed at a sufficient distance, the upward thrust dominates. This is not to say that we are dealing with a simple algebraic sum of pluses and minuses, of ascending and descending movements wherein the former dominate. Often it is from the struggle between opposite tendencies, from the opposition of contraries, that progress arises. Synthesis implies analysis, composition, decomposition. The *struggle for life* selects successful variations. The adapting Ego arises from conflicts between instinct and the external demands of society or those introjected in the Superego. "The perfect life of the spirit," St. John of the Cross tells us, "is achieved by the mortification of all the vices and all the appetites of nature itself in its entirety." Old Heraclitus was not mistaken in thinking that contradiction is good, war universal and combat the justice and source of everything; that in his prayer for peace Homer was praying unwittingly for the destruction of the world.[15, 16] But battles can be good or bad, and there are other vehicles for progress.

Notable among the latter are analysis and synthesis "in the mind." Analysis does not necessarily destroy the real object, and synthesis does not necessarily surpass a contradiction between thesis and antithesis. Things are perceived under an ever increasing number of concomitant aspects which are consciously interrelated. Here, rather than a real "opposition" of aspects, synthesis surmounts an artificial separation between them arising from our ignorance or our prejudices. Recall those mistaken ideas, those theoretical and practical wanderings that were for so long the consequence of misunderstanding our neurophysiological and cerebral aspects.*[4, 17] The processes, at once permanent and changing, are increasingly understood as such, grasped in their totality. A translation error is responsible for the idea that Hegel proposed that the bud refutes the flower and the flower the bud: *man könnte sagen*—one could say... He clearly sees, as Bergson will do later, that the flower and the bud are but artificially isolated moments in "the organic unity of the whole,"[18] that here "the opposition between the thesis and the antithesis" is a result of ignorance, of an intellectual myopia that forces us to isolate from each other the moments and aspects of one and the same process, in order, so to speak, to "reify" them as separate entities; and that synthesis is the result of an increase in knowledge and an enlargement of vision.

The purgative way, the subject of our next inquiry, constitutes a remarkable example of conflict dialectic: the mortification of the senses and spiritual faculties designed to accommodate them to God. Nevertheless, in every case embraced by the goal and method of St. John of the Cross, the interior conflict consists only partially, momentarily, and in a qualified way in the emptying of that habitual and fruitful thought process known as the analytico-synthetic dialectic. Rather than an annihilation, what is happening here is a purification. This is not always the case in all the non-Christian ways of mysticism.

---

*Concerning "the intellectual soul," Aristotle says that "at the present time, nothing is evident." In this he shows himself more prudent than a number of his predecessors and successors. But he adds that "it may well be that here we are dealing with a very different kind of souls, one that can survive separation from the body, like the eternal from the corruptible."

CHAPTER VII

Spiritual Background

Darwin, the Buddha, Freud.

Darwin in the attachment of the dog to its all powerful master, and the Buddha and Freud in the love and admiration of the little child for its father, in its fear of him and its dependence on him, all saw therein the roots of religious feeling. To the adult the world appears still more vast, more mysterious and dangerous, and man more alone, and he tends to *project* onto Heaven his need for protection, his wanting to be reassured, and his refusal of death.

It is quite true that a number of religions manifest the desire for an all powerful Father who is in Heaven. Nevertheless, in my opinion, here again the "second topic" of Freud shows itself wanting. As much as or more than with infantile dependence, religious sentiment, even when expressed naively or inadequately, is in agreement with our irresistible propensity to understand, to love, to participate, to enter ever greater *communion*, to *locate* man, the part, ever more deeply in the All, even to the point of wanting to be united to It, identified with It, or to be dissolved in It. It is, if you will, a modality, an aspect, a moment in that tendency towards the liberty of universality whose humble beginnings we have perceived in simply physico-chemical realities and in life, and a beginning of its blossoming in man.

It is well to recall that too often we have proven impatient and superficial, we have not taken into account the gap between our desire and our knowing. Rarely have we said, in situations when indicated, "I know that

I do not know," or I do not yet know, or I do not know if I will ever know. We are too frequently satisfied with getting off cheaply, too often we encumber with myths our capacity to feel, understand, love, and hope. This is not to say that faith cannot legitimately reach beyond knowing and transcend it. Still it must be founded upon serious apologetical motives, or upon "experiences" that are neither circular, given as grounding the faith that leads to them, nor interpreted without exhausting circumspection.

Anthropoids.

Let us focus our lens on what appeared a few moments ago as the last millimeters of the meter of biological evolution, and let us once again increase the magnification. What we are now looking at is man's prehistory, with, at its outside, a minuscule sliver of history: three million years or more after the dawn of man, a few thousand years after the beginning of history, i.e., when writing first appeared.

But lower on the common trunk, a long time before this, the ancestors of our current and closest cousins, the chimpanzees, had broken off. Like many animals, ourselves included, the chimpanzees perceive and distinguish the rhythms and relations of the cosmos. Perhaps they even sacralize them in an incipient fashion. During big storms the entire tribe climbs to the top of a hill, where the females and the young sit and watch the males charge down. Aggressiveness? Defense? Attack? Projection? Introjection? Participation? Communion? Or the first roots of a *veni creator spiritus?* In any case there is no fear or terror.[19] I must limit myself to posing these questions to the admirable Madame Van Lawick-Goodall or her successors. To add just one point, again the contribution of Madame Van Lawick-Goodall, during occasional cannibalistic feasts the skulls of victims are broken open and their brains eaten, preferentially by the troop leaders. I myself, during a storm, was once struck by hearing a dog bark at each clap of thunder, without the least sign of fear. One lovely summer evening I saw another stretched out on a wall watching at length the setting of the sun... Think also of the sexual ornamentation of the males, designed to attract the females—and above all of the social instincts, the "instincts towards service," and that instinct towards seeking, towards relation, towards a seemingly disinterested interest in all beings—exhibiting the roots of aesthetics, morality, religion, and spirituality, to which Bergson did not advert.

Prehistory and protohistory.

We still do not know a great deal about the distant prehistory surrounding human spirituality, despite the fact that the latter has certainly set deep roots in it. Here and there, stones hewn on both faces with *useless beauty*;[3] human skulls gathered together, some of them pierced, possibly but not certainly for cult reasons or ritual eating; human remains annointed with red ochre, the color of blood, of life; skeletons bound and thus rendered harmless, or placed in the fetal position; burials with an easterly orientation, where each morning the sun rises; and to conclude, marvelous wall paintings for twenty thousand years, representing animals and men, depicted in hunting scenes, scenes of magic and even shamanistic ecstasy, centered upon the relationships between animals and men...

From these various fossil documents and their prudent confrontation with the behavior of hunting tribes still living now, the apparent conclusion is that our distant ancestors were beginning to "sacralize" their relations with the cosmos, with nature. I would say that with a more or less utilitarian spirit, but always with an attitude of respect and solemnity, they were beginning to *situate themselves as parts within the All and to behave accordingly.* Perhaps they adored the sun, fecundity, and when they discovered it, fire, along with the Spirit of prey and the hunt. Perhaps they had some inkling about man's beginning and end, and believed in the immortality of man.[20] They probably had the idea of identifying themselves, they themselves or their ancestors, with the animals, as did the later totemic religions[21]—right up to our modern conquerors. Rather than to the gods, armed cavalry and armored divisions setting out to pillage have chosen to compare themselves to wolf packs.

Ten thousand years ago the climate improved, the glaciers retired northward, followed by the reindeer and the hunters. Agriculture began to settle in, and with it a vegetal, cyclical notion of the cosmos and of life. Like the plants, God, the world, and man lives, dies, and knows rebirth... Soon, in Thrace or Phrygia, Dionysios emerges, from our mother the earth fecondated by the thunder, the God who dies and is reborn. Carnac, Stonehenge, and megalithic civilization "eternalized" their dead through stones placed in the ground or dressed, indestructible tombs, astonishing and ever solitary, melancholic affirmations of the union between the subterranean world, the fertile and verdant surface of the land, and the starry heavens.[22, 23, 24]

One last time let us adjust the lense and increase the magnification. Now it is the narrow sliver of written history that strikes our eyes. Rarely, here or there, ritual interdiction of writing prolonged somewhat the time of prehistory, foreshadowing the future anathemas against Gutenberg, printing, the diffusion of the Bible, then of science, the censures, indexing and all manner of autos-da-fé. A number of megaliths became the object of pious destruction, even used for building houses.

Mesopotamia.

"History begins with Sumer,"[25, 26, 27] continuing and developing its acquisition of prehistory and protohistory. Water is the primordial reality. At one and the same time man is matter, the work of wicked genies, and spiritual form willed by God. Dualism and idealism are becoming increasingly precise, at a mid-point between their prehistoric origin and their Platonic expression that continues to impregnate a large sector of modern spirituality. The destiny of man, fashioned in part of clay, is a tragic one. God, Marduk, is transcendent, far off, inaccessible. Nevertheless, through that which is spiritual within him, man is able to serve God and even cooperate with Him. But there is no question for him of divine union, still less of identification with God, even "by participation." The hero Gilgamesh does not achieve immortality.[20]

Egypt. The Mysteries of Isis and Osiris.

More compassionate towards the living and the dead are, in Egypt, Ra, the Sun God who rises in the east and sets in the west, who on Osiris' bark traverses the subterranean regions during the night and casts light upon them, and Osiris, the God of the fields, killed yet restored to life. The Pharaoh is God, or the son of God. The monumental and indestructible pyramids forever maintain open communication between the tombs of kings departed and the Sun. It is not through asceticism, but through a just and well ordered life that man after death can become, if not Osiris himself, at least conformed to Osiris, protected by him, and marked forever with his seal. The cult of Ra and that of Osiris are super-imposed upon and grounded in each other, not entirely without difficulties. The relationships between the soul and the body are not always very clear. It is felt that the soul can quit the body and then return to it, and it is arranged for the soul to pass on towards the sun while the body is being conserved and protected at the same time. At any rate, the accent is not on the duality, the heterogeneity, the separation of the soul and the body. Man continues to be *situated*. He draws closer to God.[20, 27, 28, 29]

In the Hellenistic mysteries of Isis and Osiris, not without connection with ancient religion, it is thought that the initiated can be *divinized*, can *become* Osiris-Ra or Horus, and that while still alive. The rite of initiation seems to consist of a rite of death and resurrection—of mortification and spiritual rebirth? "I have arrived at the confines of death; having tread the threshold of Prosperine I have come back borne across the elements. At midnight I have see the sun shine forth; I have been able to contemplate the gods of the underworld and the gods of the heavens face to face, and at close quarters I have adored them" (Apuleius, Met., XI, 23, as cited by Mircea Eliade).[20]

Dionysius.

Spirit of life, of vegetation and renewal, born of the earth and the thunderbolt, or of a mortal woman and God, slaughtered and restored, a young god of many forms who appears and disappears, Dionysius of the ivy crown, the clamorous one, the eater of raw flesh, *fills with his presence* his ecstatic faithful ones.

The ecstacy is achieved by means of frenetic rites, chants, dances, and cries, and the tearing apart and devouring of living animal or human victims.[20, 30, 31] With greater or lesser completeness, more or less masked, with substitutions, sublimations, and blended in with others, these ancient technics of communication, communion, union, and identification, along with all that they include of splitting, of projection, and of introjection, are still used today, and not only by Whirling Dervishes and fans of Rock and Roll and Johnny Hallyday... The experiences to which they lead are interpreted differently in different cultural contexts. Emphasis is placed upon the idea that the wisdom of men is folly in the eyes of God, that *enthusiasm, mania, ecstacy, divine possession* demand that one renounce human reason, at least for a period of time and in a certain fashion. "Are we the only ones in town who dance for Bacchus? Then we alone show good sense, while the others are delirious."[30] And according to Plato, Socrates echoes the same: "Delirium is a finer thing than good sense: divine delirium is better than good sense of human origin"[32] (Phaedrus).

Orpheus, Pythagoras, Plato, the Neo-platonics.

Greek civilization flourishes, and the influence of oriental spiritualities becomes operative. In place of savage ritual, an uncertain cosmology, and the anthropology and eschatology of the old Bacchanalian, Orphic, and Pythagorian religion, Plato and the Neo-platonics substitute more refined and more precise views, if not necessarily more true. The world here below is naught but a vague and fluctuating reflection of the eternal ideas, the body is the "tomb of the soul." The latter is immortal and committed—as the Hindus maintain—to a perpetual migration, until she *remembers* the ideal Goodness and Beauty she once contemplated and, released from the impurities of her successive bodies, *rejoins Unity.*[16, 20, 32, 33, 34, 35, 36, 37] Of all these divine deliriums, the highest, the most beautiful, and the best is *love,* comparable to that which a man of years can feel for "a young and handsome youth," and which at the same time "can be excited and exalted by him"[32] (Phaedrus). I will return to the Neo-platonics and Plotinus, who are so close at once to the Hindus, Plato,[37] and nascent Christianity.

India.

"There is no happiness in something small and finite. *Only the infinite can provide us with happiness"* (Chândogya Upanishad, VII, 23). "You are that, between your soul and the cosmic soul there is an identity. Think no more, speak no more, acknowledge that identity" (Chândogya Upanishad, VI, 9, 1–3).

The Swami Nityabodhânanda—who is also familiar with two thousand years of Christian civilization—summarizes and comments upon that quintessence of Hindu thought as follows: "You are that (you are part and parcel of the totality) is a call for each of us to be aware of unity within diversity." "Your self is identical with the Supreme Self," the "Atman" with the "Brahman," and in terms that are almost Christian, "Lord, I adore you through my total belonging to you. I belong to you. You belong to me."[2] A little more stress on immanence, with less on intolerance, and these might be the words of St. John of the Cross.[38] Like Platonism and Neo-platonism in particular, like Christian spirituality, especially of the school of St. John, Hindu spirituality emphasizes the ways to "purity," detachment, and self effacement, to the very point of abandoning our normal ways of feeling and thinking. Disencumbering, purgation of "nothings," spiritual emptying are the pre-requisites for being invaded by the All. Yoga[40]—and why not modern "relaxation?"[41, 42, 43]—is but one of these purgative and unitive methods. When the individual self has experienced identity with the absolute Self here below, and when this continues to the moment of death, the human soul is dissolved in the All and returns no more. Otherwise it remains prisoner to the cycle of perpetual rebirth.

A.C. Bhaktivedanta Swâmi Prabhupâda, the eminent representative of the bhakti tendency, which stresses the spiritual love and the personal (though always immanent, or at once immanent and transcendent) character of the divinity, interprets as follows verse 20 of the Srîmad Bhâgavatam, "the mature fruit of the tree of the vedas": "…there is a growing belief, especially in India, that *man, by the force of austerity, can become God.*" Inversely, God, in His Recreations, Emanations, Manifestations, and Avatars, makes Himself worlds and men, without ever ceasing for all that to remain at peace, at rest, Himself.[39]

Buddhism.

Offspring of Hinduism, the Buddha, *the awakened one,* also encouraged *detachment,* although through ascetical ways that were less extreme, less "physical' than those which the spiritual Hindus sometimes used and which he himself used before his awakening. For him there is neither God, nor Atman, nor Brahman, nor any individual self identical with a cosmic Self, nor any blissful eternal life. Transmigration of souls is not placed in question. Man is alone. He is nothing but an ephemeral nexus of variable and conditioned relations, a single moment in a chain of suffering existences. Nirvâna is achieved through the renunciation of ego desires, even those of existing and becoming. It consists in final *extinction,* in the cessation of perpetual rebirths. But before disappearing, the buddha, the arahant "radiates universal benevolence, compassion, joyful sympathy, and equanimity."[44]

For the modern unbeliever, such final extinction is obvious, and for him there can be another way of making sense of life and death.

Other Spiritualities.

We should also speak about Shamanism and the ancient technics for arousing ecstacy,[45] about the shamans' death and resurrection symbolism, their mystical voyages to Hell and Heaven, and their ascents of the Cosmic Tree. And about the religions, wisdoms, and spiritualities of the African, the Chinese, Japanese, American Indian, Jew, Mussulman, Orthodox, Hesychast, Protestant...;[20, 38, 46] about Plotinus, Master Eckart and the Rhine mystics,[47] St. Francis of Assisi, the little brother of the stars, of the sun, moon, earth, plants and animals,[48] as well as the Iranian evolution, with its growing contempt for "matter" and "flesh" which will end with the Manichaean opposition between the two Creators, one good and the other evil, and their two creations, the spiritual and divine, and the material and diabolical;[20, 27] and about Gnosticism.[49]

We ought to recall emphatically that spirituality is by no means a stranger to modern forms of atheism. Marx, an heir to the more cultural than racial Indo-europeanism of German romanticism, was one with Heraclitus and the Buddha in maintaining that reality is nothing but change, and never can the same person bathe twice in the same river. The individual amounts to little, the collectivity is what matters. Liberty is necessity once understood, accepted, willed, at least the necessity of the moment. Detachment, love of neighbor, happiness take the route of production and the collective ownership of the means of production. As for consuming societies, founded or not on the profit motive, linked or not to the imperative of maximum profit, along with many inessential and dispersive goods, they are quite capable of furnishing a material base for spiritual progress. They may lack neither the spirit of service nor the liberty of universality.[4]

And above all we ought not to forget that man, "the apex of evolution and revolutions,"[4] sinks his roots deep among the beasts, and that here are the origins, the first awakenings, the first "sources of morality, religion, and spirituality," embracing among others the instincts of conservation, of growth and reproduction, the social instincts, and, we repeat, that "realistic" instinct of relation, a kind of disinterested interest in that which is other than the self. These are instincts which will soon join hands with intelligence...

CHAPTER VIII

St. John of the Cross

The Old and New Testaments.

"In the beginning of creation, when God made heaven and earth, the earth was without form and void, with darkness over the face of the abyss, and a mighty wind that swept over the surface of the waters" (Genesis, 1:1–2).[50] Here we have an ancient cosmological theme which will gain precision in the notion of creation *ex nihilo* by the Word. Creation does not result from a contest between Good and Evil.[20] It is the consequence of a superabundance of divine love. Out of clay and the breath of His mouth, God creates man *according to His own image,* bestows *liberty* on him, i.e., the power to disobey Him, to refuse Him, and cast him out of the earthly paradise for having misused that liberty in choosing to taste the forbidden fruit of the tree of the knowledge of good and evil. "The Lord God said: the man has become like one of us, knowing good and evil; what if he now reaches out his hand and takes fruit from the tree of life also, eats it and lives forever?" (Genesis, 3:22). He punishes man a second time for his wickedness, wiping out all life under the deluge, with the exception of Noah the just and some plants and animals in the Ark. Then man tried to scale the heavens and God destroyed the Tower of Babel, and He set up misunderstanding between men by diversity of languages as a prelude to giving his apostles, along with the Holy Spirit, the gift of tongues and the mission to teach all the peoples of the earth. He restores sinful humanity by the incarnation, passion, and resurrection of His dearly beloved Son—a very ancient cosmological theme also—initiates the reign of love, and, with it, the Kingdom of Heaven that begins on earth, the resurrection of the body, and eternal life. *Ama et fac quod vis.* Once again man is *situated:* like all creatures created *ex nihilo,* made in the image of God, free to accept or to refuse God and with Him the fullness of being, free to do good or evil—the latter being no more than something missing, "a hole in being"[51]— able to unite with God here below through love and after death to contemplate Him eternally in beatitude and glory.

The Jews who were waiting for a temporal Messiah and the Romans, who feared revolutionaries, condemn Jesus and crucify him. A few centuries later Mohammed sets monotheism on a different path. Space and time do not permit an adequate treatment of the admirable spiritualities of Judaism and Islam, nor of Neo-platonism, so close in certain ways to Christianity then in its infancy, some other "mystery religions," and Hindu mysticism.[37, 52] I might just allow myself to add that Greek influence, and particularly that of Parmenides, perhaps led the authors of the Septuagint into an erroneous translation. It is possible that the God of the Hebrews named himself "I am He who is becoming" and not "I am He who is," which is the basis of Christian belief and philosophy.

What of archaic and foreign influences? A chance encounter between a volcano god and the remembrance of Aton conserved and transmitted by Moses?[53] A longing for the Father? A desire to live eternally? An infantile attempt at omnipotence? A split and external deflection of the "ego"? A projection outside of ourselves, into an illusory Heaven, of infinite aspirations and possibilities that we feel or believe we feel within us? A desire to be conformed to an idealized image of ourselves, to become what we are, what we are capable of being or believe we are capable of being? An opiate dispensed cheaply to the poor by the wealthy? A groundwork for temporal power? A progressive revelation gradually drawing together again partial truths dissipated by original sin or gradually arising out of animality? A manifestation, under more or less aberrant forms, of an authentic and profound tendency towards the liberty of universality?

We limit ourselves to the observation that St. John of the Cross, a Carmelite of the golden age of untamed, proud, radical, and magnificent Spain—a *combative* race—inscribed his spiritual itinerary within the framework of the Catholic faith, "a proportionate and proximate means" of loving union with God. This is the religion that gave form to his hope and his charity. Perhaps under other formation his ardent love would have lifted him to other peaks. Be that as it may, his experience, as I will try to show, is not without universal value.

The Degrees of Knowing.

St. John of the Cross had attended the University of Salamanca and was formed in part by the Dominicans of the school of Aristotle and St. Thomas Aquinas. Thus for him man here below has the capacity to know something about God. This knowing is inseparable from action, from passion even, and above all from love. It possesses degrees.[54]

In natural theology it is "the God of the philosophers"[55] which is deduced or induced from his works, his creatures, man, particularly the "interior man," created by him in his image. Their proofs of the existence of God seem convincing and compelling to the natural theologian. But for all that he does not spurn what Maritain calls the subjective comforts of faith. The latter can indicate objects available for reason's reflection that it may otherwise not have considered; and a living faith can favorably dispose the philosopher for research.[56]

Philosophers thinking, rightly or wrongly, that they have demonstrated the existence of God and know something about Him, or simple faithful, through *faith,* the common knowledge of believers, we hold that we learn about God himself speaking to us personally as He did to Moses, or through the mouth of the prophets, or that of His Son, or through the Holy Spirit who seized the Apostles on the day of Pentecost, something intimate about the life of the Trinity, "mysteries hidden since the world began."

Faith would not be contrary to reason, but higher than it. It would not reject the support of experimental and rational apologetics, the motives of believableness (or unbelievableness of different or contrary beliefs). It would be imperfect, partial, analogical, proportionate to our smallness in the face of God. "With the grace of God" it would nevertheless lead here below to a more intimate relationship with the divinity. Human nature, with its possibilities, its desires and its fears, cultural background, environment, education, and example doubtlessly play a greater role in the matter of faith than does philosophy.

Finally, somewhere between a faith still filled with human images and limited, limiting concepts, and the beatific vision reserved for the just after their death, there would be a possibility, starting here below, of having a more direct, more intimate contact with God, even though still achieved through the veil of faith. God would allow himself to be glimpsed fleetingly at the very time when man would begin to assume *divinity,* divinity "not by nature, clearly, but by participation."[57]   "The life I live is not my life," cries out St. Paul, "but the life which Christ lives in me."[50]

The purgative way.

For St. John of the Cross, as for a multitude of other Christian or non-Christian mystics, the way to arrive at unity with God starting here below is simple, rigorous, and "crucifying." It consists in uprooting everything in us that can obstruct, retard, lessen, or hinder that union. "If you stop at some one thing, you do not cast yourself upon the All" *(The Ascent,* I, 15). "Whosoever will have learned to die to all shall have life in all" *(Maxims).*

Sin is not all that can become an obstacle: the spiritual person, the "advanced" whom St. John of the Cross is addressing, have long since overcome sin. It is everything in us that is disproportionate to God. It is all those "partial goods," as good as they can be in their proper order and degree, to the extent that our attachment to them can blind us, bind us, and prevent us from "casting ourselves upon the All." The mystical nights are these purifications of the senses and of the spirit, "active" nights when man begins, "passive" when God continues and accomplishes.

The active purification of the senses.

"The senses—*el sentido"* is taken by St. John of the Cross very broadly. Included also are imagination, sense memory, and the discursive operations of intelligence working with the data of the senses.

The spiritual person will first work at mortifying his appetites and to begin with "will refuse satisfactions of the sense order which might include some sin or lead to it, right down to the least simply imperfect and superfluous satisfactions which could encumber his flight towards God":[58] *un gustillo*—a small satisfaction of the tongue—an *asimiantillo*— a small attachment—, *conversacionillas*—petty, useless conversations... For "it is all the same if a bird be restrained by a light or by a heavy tether; be it only a simple thread, until it breaks it the bird will remain bound and will be unable to take flight" *(Maximes).*

Then he will strip his spiritual faculties—the intelligence, the intellectual memory, the will—of all sense support, because, in a way, the senses are disproportionate to God, the ineffable, the unutterable, who is formless and without image.

To introduce the senses actively into their night is to begin rendering them naked and empty—*desnudez y vacio*—in order to attune them to the spirit, and then both to God: "The gate that leads to life is small and the road is narrow…" (Matthew, 7:14); "He next says that the road is narrow—that is to say, the road of perfection—in order to make it clear that, to travel upon the road of perfection, the soul has not only to enter by the strait gate, emptying itself of things of sense, but that it has also to constrain itself, freeing and disencumbering itself completely in that which pertains to the spirit" *(The Ascent,* II, 7, p. 88).

The active purification of the spirit.

Like the night of the senses accommodating them to the spirit, the active night of the spirit is a free act of asceticism designed to purify the spirit for its accommodation to God. Through this purification, the faculties of the spirit begin to be disposed to the three theological virtues: the intellect to faith, the memory to hope, and the will to charity, i.e., to love. Here again there is no question of renouncing only "sins of the spirit," and "disordered appetites of our spiritual faculties," but equally as well "appetites that are simply natural, no matter how good they are in their own order, in so far as they are not entirely related to God and, in some way or another, hinder union with God."[58]

Faith and the active purification of the intellect.

Through its active purification, its free act of asceticism, *el entendimiento,* the intellect begins to be disposed to faith. "Faith, say the theologians, is a habit of the soul, certain and *obscure.* And the reason for its being an obscure habit is that it makes us believe truths revealed by God Himself, which transcend all natural light, and exceed all human understanding, beyond all proportion. Hence it follows that, for the soul, this excessive light of faith which is given to it is thick darkness…for it is by blinding that it gives light, according to (the) saying of Isaiah" *(Ascent* II, 3, p.70–72). Intelligence, and faith along with it, must undergo a progressive stripping away of every "particular and distinct image, figure, form, representation, and conception of God," because these are all disproportionate to God. In Book two of *The Ascent of Mount Carmel,* chapters seven to twenty-six are consecrated to a minute examination of all the sense elements, and all the "clear, distinct, and particular" concepts that faith must clear away. When faith is totally purified, once it has become "general and obscure," it will flower into the highest form of contemplation, and into the union of love with God.

Though requisite for mystical union, this purified intelligence and this general and obscure faith nevertheless contradict neither reason, faith, prayer, nor "discursive" meditation. Even though encumbered with words and images, faith, so long as it is sincere and informed by an ardent charity, suffices for sanctity here below and a blissful life after death. To put it simply, once he has taken all the fruits possible from prayer and discursive meditation, the spiritual person must abandon them for infused contemplation, which consists of the experience of God in inner silence and emptiness. St. John of the Cross explains at great length in his *Ascent of Mount Carmel,* resuming the same theme in his *Maxims,* the signs by which one knows that this moment has come: "The signs of interior recollection are three; first, if the soul has no pleasure in transitory things; second, if it have pleasure in solitude and silence and give heed to all that leads to greater perfection; third, if the things which were wont to help it (such as considerations, meditations, and acts) now hinder it and the soul has no other support in prayer than faith and charity." *(Spiritual Sentences and Maxims,* p. 253). He is indignant at bad directors who "think that these souls are idle. And therefore they disturb and impede the peace of this quiet and hushed contemplation which God has been giving their penitents by His own power..." *(Living Flame of Love,* pp. 189–190).

Hope and the active purification of the memory.

To hope is to tend confidently towards a good that is not yet possessed. The essential function of the memory, informed by hope, is to bear the goal in mind constantly, which is God, and "the more the soul rejoices in any other thing than God, the less completely will it centre its rejoicing in God" *(Ascent,* III, 16, pp. 259–260). Not only should memory and hope be freed from that multitude of worthless objects that bind and blind them, or at the very least distract and diffuse them, but—at least as far as their ordinations towards God is concerned—they should also be emptied of images, of con-

cepts and words, which, St. John of the Cross repeatedly insists, are disproportionate to God: "(the emptying) cannot happen unless the memory be
annihilated as to all its forms, if it is to be united with God....for God comes
beneath no definite form or kind of knowledge whatsoever, as we have said
in treating of the night of the understanding" *(Ascent,* III, 2, p.227).

Charity and the active purification of the will.

"We should have accomplished nothing by the purification of the understanding in order to ground it in the virtue of faith, and by the purgation of
the memory in order to ground it in hope, if we purged not the will also
according to the third virtue, which is charity, whereby the works that are
done in faith live and have great merit, and without it are of no worth. For, as
St. James says; "Without works of charity, faith is dead" (James, 2:20.
Ascent, III, 16, pp.258–259). "You must love the Lord your God with all
your heart and soul and strength" (Deuteronomy, 6:5). "O my strength, to
thee I turn in the night-watches; for thou, O God, art my strong tower. My
God, in his true love, shall be my champion" (Psalm 59, 9–10). To be able to
tend entirely towards God, the will in its turn must be purified of every tendency that is directly contrary, or simply distracting or diffusing... "And, to
the end that the soul might do this, we shall treat of the purgation from the
will of all its unruly affections, whence arise unruly operations, affections
and desires, and whence also arises its failure to keep all its strength for God.
These affections and passions are four, namely: joy, hope, grief, and fear"
(Ascent, III, 16, p. 259). The last thirty chapters of the Ascent of Mount
Carmel (unfinished) pass in review the different kinds of goods—"partial
goods"—in which the will can place its joy and so perish: "Joy may arise
from six kinds of good things or blessings, namely: temporal, natural, sensual, moral, supernatural and spiritual. Of these we shall speak in their order,
controlling the will with regard to them so that it may not be encumbered by
them and fail to place the strength of its joy in God" *(Ascent,* III, 17, p. 262).

Once it has been entirely purified, the human will simply becomes one
with the will of God—*hecha una cosa con la voluntad de Dios*—an
expression that reoccurs constantly under the pen of St. John of the Cross.
Once the "interior man," the spiritual man, is completely purged of all
human pettiness and filled with the Holy Spirit, he himself is transformed
into a living flame of love to the very point of becoming divine by participation—*hecho Dios amor por participacion*—, a leitmotiv and earthly

objective in St. John, as a prelude to eternal beatitude. But it is the daily prayer of all Christians as well: "Thy will be done..."

Passive purification.

By the "passive" or "dark night"—because here the darkness is thickest— St. John of the Cross understands the trials that the spiritual person receives from God with the purpose of disposing him for the transforming union of love. "I am the real vine, and my Father is the gardener. Every barren branch of mine he cuts away; and every fruiting branch he cleans, to making it more fruitful still" (John, 15: 1–2). This fruit of which he speaks is the mystical union, the participation in the divine life: *Vivo autem, jam non ego; vivit vero in me Christus,* "...the life I now live is not my life, but the life which Christ lives in me..." (Gal., 2:20). Introduced into their respective nights through voluntary asceticism, the senses and spiritual faculties now come, "if, when, and how He wills," to be ordered by Him directly to the ultimate purifications.

Following upon discursive, sense-perceptible prayer and meditation comes "acquired" or "active" contemplation, a kind of synthetic and simplified résumé of the former which already suppresses images and presages passive or "infused" contemplation and divine union. "The action of God, in its initial stage when it is weak, will interfere with every personal, discursive process, and it will end up by arresting the process completely when it is strong,"[58] thus bringing about the emptying of the senses and the human spirit of "all that is less than God." If you will permit me a more prosaic comparison than those used by John of the Cross (and after him, sometimes with less success, Father Hondet), but one that is more modern, more technical: initially a space craft propels itself by its own activity, pushing against gravity by means of its engines. Once it is free, the module no longer propels itself by its own activity but is moved by universal gravity. The latter force would be hindered if, following an error in calculation, the first stages did not separate on time and their engines continued to function...

The passive purification of the senses.

The senses—the external and internal senses, sense memory, imagination, and emotion, the sensible "matter" of discursive reasoning as it employs images and words in proceeding from *un acto a otro acto,* from one particular, distinct and limited concept to another—these should be attuned to the spirit in such fashion as not to interfere with its thrust towards God. Indeed, the transforming union of love proceeds *de puro Espiritu a espiritu puro,* from pure Spirit to purified spirit—a leitmotiv in the works of John of the Cross as well—and the purification of the spirit begins with that of sensibility, while contributing to it at the same time.

"The deprivation of sense consolations in prayer and meditation, and in the service of God in general, which are good in their own order and time, is designed to accommodate the soul to the purely spiritual in emptying it of all that is not proportionate to God."[58] Begun through voluntary asceticism, passively carried on by the divine action in us, the night of the senses becomes more obscure, the privation more terrible, but, "never suppressing without replacing with something better," God even then touches us with a sense of his ineffable presence. "Already there is a beginning of infused contemplation that causes the dark night of the senses, contributing to the mystical barrenness which actually grounds it, to the difficulty or inability to pray discursively and to the deprivation of sense joys..." while at the same time it gives as it were "a foretaste of more perfect operations, of the more spiritual joys of loving union with God."[58]

The passive purification of the spirit.

The dark night of the senses is only the "entrance and beginning" of passive, infused, and unitive contemplation: *Solo es puerta y principio de contemplacion.* "For (this dark night leads) to the purgation of the spirit, which, as we have likewise said, serves rather to accommodate sense to spirit than to unite spirit with God" *(Dark Night,* 2, p. 400). The senses themselves will achieve purification contemporaneously with the spirit, "for the imperfections and disorders of the sensual part have their strength and root in the spirit, ...wherefore... both parts of the soul are purged together." *(Dark Night,* 3, p. 403).

In these ultimate purifications, the human soul remains passive, simply accepting and submitting to the action of the Holy Spirit, blinded at first by Him "even as the eyes of the bat with regard to the sun" (Aristotle, in *Ascent,* II, 8, p.97), at first "exuding its humors" like burning wood before being transformed into fire. It is "the struggle between contraries, which cannot coexist in the same subject," an agony, *ni mas ni menos que un purgatorio,* but already a part of "the tranquil night, at the time of the rising of the dawn"—*la noche sosegada en par de los levantes de la aurora (Spiritual Canticle,* Stanza 15)—the veil of faith waxes transparent, God begins to allow himself to be glimpsed, and the man of the spirit to become, through, in, and like God, a living flame of love. *God is light...God is love* (I John, 1:5, and 4:16).

The transforming union of love.

"What God communicates to the soul in this close union is totally ineffable, unspeakable—as it is impossible to say something about God that would be similar to Him" *(Spiritual Canticle,* Stanza XVII, p. 102). St. John of the Cross adds that, however briefly, it is necessary to have experienced these privileged moments in order to understand what he wants to tell us, or rather *suggest* to us, stammering—*balbuciando*—, multiplying comparisons and symbols, repeating, diversifying, intermingling, and enriching themes as in an incantation, a litany, a counterpoint, as in a grand and marvelous poem in verse and in prose worthy of the title that his compatriots would later award him, that of "the greatest poet of Spain." Mystics or not, let us continue listening to him, seeking silence within ourselves.

> *¡Oh cauterio suave!*
> *¡Oh regalada llaga!*
> *¡Oh mano blanda!*
> *Oh toque delicado*
> *que a vida eterna sabe.*
> *¡y toda deuda paga!*
> *Matando muerte en vida la has*
> *trocado*.*

> *Oh, sweet burn! Oh, delectable wound! Oh, soft hand! Oh, delicate touch! That savours of eternal life and pays every debt. In slaying, thou hast changed death into life.*
>
> *(Living Flame of Love, Stanza II)*

---

* The music of a poem exists only in the language in which it was written. For this reason these few extracts from the poetry of John of the Cross are cited in Spanish, followed by the translation of E. Allison Peers.

Sweet burn. This refers to "the Holy Spirit, for, as Moses says in Deuteronomy, *our Lord God is a consuming fire*—that is, a fire of love" (Deuteronomy, in *Living Flame,* Stanza II, p. 141). These are the flames of Pentecost which "descended with great vehemence and enkindled the disciples...burning not but giving splendor; consuming not but enlightening" (Acts, 2:3 and the Roman Breviary for Matins of Pentecost Sunday, in *Living Flame,* Stanza II, p. 142). "Oh, delectable wound, oh, soft hand" "Thou hast wounded me, oh, hand divine, in order to heal me, and thou hast slain in me that which would have slain me but for the life of God wherein now I see that I live." "This divine touch has neither bulk nor weight, for the Word, who effects it, is far removed from any kind of mode and manner, and free from any kind of weight, of form, figure or accident...and therefore touches most subtly, lovingly, eminently and delicately" *(Living Flame,* II, pp. 147–150).

In slaying, thou hast changed death into life This verse and its commentary by St. John of the Cross, which I am going to take the liberty to cite at some length, constitutes a summary of "sanjuanism." "With respect to the spirit, there are two kinds of life; one is beatific, which consists in seeing God, and this is to be obtained by means of the natural death of the body..." "We know that if this our house of clay be dissolved, we have a dwelling of God in the heavens" (St. Paul, II Cor., 5:1, in *Living Flame,* II, p. 157). *"The other is perfect spiritual life,* which is the possession of God through the union of love, and this is attained through the complete mortification of all the vices and desires of the soul's entire nature." "If ye live according to the flesh ye shall die; but if with the spirit ye mortify the deeds of the flesh, ye shall live" (St. Paul, Romans, 8:13). "It must be known then that that which the soul here calls death is all that is meant by the "old man": namely, the employment of the faculties—memory, understanding, and will—and the use and occupation of them in things of the world, and in the desires and pleasures taken in created things. All this is the exercise of the old life, which is the death of the new, or spiritual life... as the Apostle warns us when he says that we should put off the old man and put on the new man, which according to the omnipotent God is created in righteousness and holiness (St. Paul, Ephesians, 4:22 and 24). In this new life, which begins when the soul has reached this perfection of union with God...all the desires of the soul and its faculties according to its inclinations and operations, which of themselves were the operation of death and the privation of spiritual life, *are changed into Divine opera-*

tions...thus its death has been changed into life—which is to say that animal life has been changed into spiritual life."

"For the *understanding,* which before this union understood in a natural way with the strength and vigour of its natural light, by means of the bodily senses, is now moved and informed by another and a higher principle, that of the supernatural light of God, and, the senses having been set aside, it has thus been changed into the Divine, for through union *its understanding and that of God are now both one.* And the *will,* which aforetime loved after a low manner, that of death, and with its natural affection, has now been changed into the life of divine love...moved by the power and strength of the Holy Spirit in Whom it now lives the life of love, since, through this union, *its will and His will are now only one.* And the *memory,* which of itself perceived only figures and phantasms of created things, has become changed so that it has in mind the eternal years spoken of by David. And the *natural desire,* which had only the capacity and strength to enjoy creature pleasures that work death, is now changed so that it tastes and enjoys that which is Divine... And finally, *all the movements and operations* which the soul had aforetime, and which belonged to the principle and strength of its natural life, are now in this movement changed into divine movements, dead to their operation and inclination and alive to God...even as S. Paul teaches, saying: That they that are moved by the Spirit of God are sons of God Himself (Romans, 8:14). So, as has been said, the understanding of this soul is now the understanding of God; and its will is the will of God; and its memory is the memory of God; and its delight is the delight of God; and the Substance of this soul, *although it is not the Substance of God,* ...is nevertheless united in Him and absorbed in Him, *and is thus God by participation in God...* Wherefore the soul may very well say with S. Paul: I live, yet not I but Christ liveth in me" (Gal., 2:20). "...*Absorpta est mors in victoria* (I Cor., 15:54)...death is swallowed up, victory is won." *(Living Flame,* Stanza II, pp. 157–159).

In the Spiritual Canticle, a dialog between the soul and the Bridegroom—*canciones entre el alma y el Esposo*—St. John of the Cross sings of the transforming union of love in terms of nuptial symbolism. This should not make for any illusions, no more than filial symbolism. Used in the Canticle of Canticles and then by Christian mystics of both sexes, it is particularly suited to suggest the union of love, divine activity and human passivity and receptivity—at least in a time when women were submissive to their husbands... As for the almost total absence of any reference to Marian piety, in my opinion this is explained by St. John of the Cross' desire to go to God directly. We can read the Canticle without uneasiness or reservation. *El alma,* moreover, is a feminine substantive in Spanish, *el* replacing *la* for reasons of euphony.

Alli me dio su pecho,
alli me enseñó ciencia muy
  sabrosa,
y yo le di de hecho
a mi, sin dejar cosa;
alli le prometi de ser su esposa.

There he gave me his breast; There he taught me a science
most delectable; And I gave myself to him, indeed, reserving nothing;
There I promised him to be his bride.

(Spiritual Canticle, Stanza XVIII)

The delectable science is "mystical theology—the secret science of God, which spiritual men call contemplation; this is most delectable since it is science through love." *And I gave myself to him, indeed, reserving nothing:* "God grants it in the said union, the purity and perfection which are necessary for this; for, inasmuch as He transforms the soul into Himself, He makes it to be wholly His and empties it of all that it possessed and that was alien from God." *There I promised to be His bride:* "For even as the maiden that is betrothed sets not her love upon another than her Spouse, nor directs her thoughts or her actions to any other, even so the soul in this estate has no longer any affections of the will or acts of knowledge of the understanding, nor any thought or action that is not wholly turned to God, together with its desires. *It is, as it were, Divine and deified,* so that in even its first movements it has naught whereto the will of God is opposed, in so far as it can understand" *(Spiritual Canticle,* Stanza XVIII, p. 110).

Knowledge is insufficient for divine union. *Love* is necessary. "So that, whether its exercise be with temporal things, or whether its exercise be concerning spiritual things, a soul in this case can ever say: For now my exercise is in loving alone" *Ni va tengo otro officio, que va sólo en amar es mi ejercicio (Spiritual Canticle,* Stanza XIX, p. 113).

Cuando tú me mirabas
su gracia en mi tus ojos

imprimian;
por eso me adamabas,
y en eso merecian
Los mios adorar lo que
  en ti veian.

When thou didst look on me, Thine eyes imprinted upon me thy grace;
For this cause didst thou love me greatly, Whereby mine eyes deserved
to adore what they saw in thee.

(Spiritual Canticle, Stanza XXIII)

God loves naught apart from Himself... Wherefore for God to love the soul is for Him to set it, after a certain manner, in Himself, making it equal to Himself, and thus He loves the soul in Himself, with the same love wherewith He loves Himself" *(Spiritual Canticle,* Stanza XXIII, p. 126).

Entrada se ha la esposa
en el ameno huerto deseado,
y a su sabor reposa,
el cuello reclinado
sobre los dulces brazos
  del Amado.

The Bride has entered Into the pleasant garden of her desire,
And at her pleasure rests, Her neck reclining on the gentle arms of
the Beloved.

Spiritual Canticle, Stanza XXVII)

In his commentary on this couplet, St. John of the Cross once again summarizes, magisterially, his spiritual itinerary: mortification, then spiritual betrothal and marriage: "the soul is made Divine and becomes God by participation, in so far as may be in this life, and this is the loftiest estate which in this life is attainable. For even as in the consummation of marriage according to the flesh the two become one flesh, as says the Divine Scripture, (Genesis, 2:24) even so, when this spiritual marriage between God and the soul is consummated, there are two natures in one spirit and love of God"... The bride "has gone out from all that is temporal and from all that is natural, and from all spiritual manners and modes and affections, and, having left behind and forgotten all temptations, dis-

turbances, griefs, anxiety and cares, is transformed in this lofty embrace...
(Spiritual Canticle, Stanza XXVII, p. 140).

> *...en solidad la guia*
> *a solas si querido...*

> *And in solitude her dear one alone guides her...*
>   *(Spiritual Canticle,* Stanza XXXIV)

"This signifies: In that solitude which the soul has with respect to all things and wherein she is alone with God, He guides and moves her and raises her to Divine things—that is to say, He raises her understanding to Divine intelligence, since it is now alone and detached from all other alien and contrary intelligence; and He moves her will freely to the love of God, for it is now alone and free from other affections; and He fills her memory with Divine knowledge, since it, too, is now alone and emptied of other imaginings and fancies. For as soon as the soul disencumbers these faculties and voids them of all lower things and of all attachment, leaving them in solitude with naught else—*desnudez y vacio*—God at once uses them for the invisible and Divine, and it is God Who guides the soul in this solitude, even as S. Paul says concerning the perfect: *Qui spiritu Dei aguntur,* etc. (Romans, 8:14). That is: They are moved by the Spirit of God; which is the same as saying: In solitude He guides her..." *(Spiritual Canticle,* pp.161–162);... Thus there is "fulfilled that which was promised by the Son of God—namely that, *if any man loved Him,* the Holy Spirit would come within him and would abide and dwell in him. (John, 14: 23) And this comes to pass when the understanding is divinely illumined in the wisdom of the Son, and the will is made glad in the Holy Spirit, and the Father, with His power and strength, absorbs the soul in the embrace and abyss of His sweetness..." "giving me Divine intelligence according to the ability and capacity of my understanding, and communicating love to me according to the utmost power of my will, and delighting me...with the torrent of thy delight, in thy Divine contact and substantial union, according to the utmost purity of my substance and the capacity and freedom of my memory... Inasmuch as the soul has been well purged with respect to its substance and to its faculties...the Divine Substance...absorbs it in a profound and subtie and sublime manner; and in that absorption of the soul in wisdom, the Holy Spirit brings to pass the glorious vibrations of His flame..." *(Living Flame,* Stanza I, pp. 126–127).

Thus ends here below, in anticipation of eternal beatitude, the happy adventure—*dichosa ventura*—of the soul in its quest for God: "It will find deliverance from the devil, the world, and its own sensibility…and, having obtained the precious liberty of the Spirit…it climbs from the depths to the heights. Its earthiness becomes heavenly, its humanity divine…"

The recovery of creatures.

The mortification of the "flesh," of "nature," the extreme purification, the nights of the senses and of the spirit, required, St. John of the Cross tells us, for divine union, could lead us to believe in a contempt for the world judged illusory or evil in the manner of a number of Hindu spiritual adepts, of Buddhists, Manicheans, and, closer to us, Platonists and Neoplatonists. This view would be in conformity with neither the Catholic tradition, nor Carmelite spirituality. Christians believe that God created the world out of love, made man in his own image, and judged His creation to be good (Genesis, 1:1–26).

Orientals and Greeks, according to J.A. Cuttat, do not conceive of the world as a created reality, i.e., as having been "contrived" out of nothing by a God who pre-exists it and then brings it gradually into realization. For them creation is rather the perpetual reflection of a co-existing Eternity, or as an immemorial "image," albeit a fleeting and imperfect one, of a blissful and impassive Reality existing in perfect contentment. In a word, as manifestation the universe is an inevitable degradation; as creation it is a providential becoming. The "Continuous Return" of Chinese Taoism, the Buddhist "Round of Existence" *(samsâra),* the "Cycles of Brahma manifestation" (described as the divine "magician" setting up *maya* or "universal illusion") and the Greek *Cosmos* are themselves illusory and "deifuge"; freely endowed by its author with its own reality, the universe of the Bible has a divine vocation. This is why the revelation of Abraham, in place of the reversible and "cyclical" time of the extra-biblical cosmologies, the perpetual alternating of the "days and nights of Brahma" where the cosmic process is a fatal estrangement from the divine, substituted irreversible time, "linear" and theocentric, in which creation as such, conceived and prefigured in the "six days"of Genesis, is to the contrary a progressive ascent, through man, towards the Creator. Inaugurating the *valorization of time,* the Old Testament revealed the world as *history*.[38, 59]

¡Oh bosques y espesuras,
plantadas por la mano del
  Amado!
¡Oh prado de verduras
de flores esmaltado!
Decid si por vosotros ha
  pasado.

Respuesta de las criaturas

Mil gracias derramando
pasó por estos sotos con
  presura,
Y, yéndolos mirando,
con sola su figura
vestidos los dejó de
  hermosura.

O woods and thickets Planted by the hand of the Beloved!
O meadow of verdure, enamelled with flowers, say if he has
passed by you.

Answer of the creatures

Scattering a thousand graces, He passed through these groves
in haste, And, looking upon them as he went, Left them, by his glance
alone, clothed with beauty.

(Spiritual Canticle, Stanzas IV and V)

After "courage not to turn aside after delights and pleasures, and fortitude to conquer temptations and difficulties, wherein consists the practice of *self-knowledge, which is the first thing that the soul must achieve in order to come to the knowledge of God...* consideration of the creatures is the first thing in order upon this spiritual road to the knowledge of God; by means of them the soul considers His greatness and excellence, according to that word of the Apostle where he says: *Invisibilia enim ipsius a creatura mundi, per ea quae facta sunt intellecta conspiciuntur.* Which is as much to say: The invisible things of God are known by the soul through the invisible and created visible things (St. Paul, Romans, 1:20)... God looked at all things in this image of His Son alone, which was to give them their natural being, to communicate to them many natural gifts and graces, and to make them finished and perfect, even as He says in Genesis, in these words: God saw all the things that He had made and they were very good (Genesis, 1:31)... And not only did he communicate to them their being and their natural graces...but also in this image of His Son alone He left them clothed with beauty... with marvelous natural virtue and beauty, derived from and communicated by that infinite supernatural beauty of the image of God, Whose beholding of them clothes the world and all the heavens with beauty and joy; just as does also the opening of His hand, whereby, as David says: *Imples omne animal benedictione.* That is to say: Thou fillest every animal with blessing (Psalm 144, 16)...but also in this image of His Son alone He left them clothed with beauty, communicating to them supernatural being. This was when he became man, and thus exalted man in the beauty of God, and consequently exalted all the creatures in him, since in uniting Himself with man He united Himself with the nature of them all. Wherefore said the same Son of God: *Si ego exaltatus a terra fuero, omnia traham ad me ipsum.* That is: I if I be lifted up from this earth, will draw all things unto me (John, 12:32)." *(Spiritual Canticle,* Stanzas IV and V, pp. 46–50).

But the mystical soul is not content with this indirect knowledge of God..."And therefore the soul being wounded in love by this trace of the beauty of her Beloved which she has known through the creatures, yearns to behold that invisible beauty which was caused by this visible beauty, and speaks in the stanza following."

¡Ay, quién podrá sanarme!
Acaba de entregarte ya de
  vero;
no quieras enviarme
de hoy más ya mensajero:
que no saben decirme lo que
  quiero.

Ah, who will be able to heal me! Surrender thou thyself now completely. From to-day do thou send me now no other messenger, For they cannot tell me what I wish.

(Spiritual Canticle, Stanza VI)

That which she desires, and that which she obtains, is to be united with God and to understand in God the creatures of God. This is, says St. John of the Cross, what the theologians call *morning* knowledge and *evening* knowledge: knowledge of God as God and knowledge of God as creator. "In that aforesaid tranquility and silence of the night, and in that knowledge of the Divine light, the soul is able to see a marvelous fitness and disposition of the wisdom of God in the diversities of all His creatures and works, all and each of which are endowed with a certain response to God... She sees that each one after its manner exalts God, since it has God in itself according to its capacity; and thus all these voices make one voice of music, extolling the greatness of God and His marvelous knowledge and wisdom... and inasmuch as the soul receives this sounding music, not without solitude and withdrawal from all outward things, she calls them the *silent music* and *the sounding solitude—la musica callada, la soledad sonora" (Spiritual Canticle,* pp. 88–90). And when the mystical union has been realized, she can say:

Gocémonos, Amado,
Y vámonos a ver en tu
  hermosura
al monte o al collado...

Let us rejoice, Beloved, And let us go to see ourselves in thy
beauty, To the mountain or the hill...

(Spiritual Canticle, Stanza XXXV)

"(May) my beauty...be Thy beauty, and Thy beauty my beauty... This is the adoption of the sons of God, who will truly say to God that which the Son Himself said through St. John to the Eternal Father, in these words: *Omnia mea tua sunt, et tua mea sunt.* Which signifies: Father, all my things are Thine and Thy things are mine. He by essence, being the Son by nature; and we by participation, being sons by adoption (John, 17:10)... *To the mountain or the hill:* This means to the knowledge of the morning, as theologians say, which is knowledge in the Divine Word, Who is here understood by the *mountain;* because the Word is the loftiest essential Wisdom of God. Or let us go to the knowledge of the evening, which is the wisdom of God in His creatures and works and wondrous ordinances; this is here signified by the *hill,* which is lower than the mountain... The soul cannot see herself in the beauty of God and be made

like to Him therein, save by being transformed in the Wisdom of God, wherein that which is above is seen and possessed; wherefore she desires to go to the mountain or to the hill" *(Spiritual Canticle,* Stanza XXXV, pp. 164–165).

The purified senses, the intelligence, memory, and will transformed into those of God, the "deep caverns" of its powers, now with a capacity for the infinite, stripped of the "nothings" that had closed off entry, are all henceforth filled with the oceanic presence of God. The human soul having arrived at "this purity and cleanness...in this state of perfection" (Spiritual Canticle, Stanza XXXVIII, p. 175) can sing with St. John of the Cross:

El aspirar de l'aire,
el canto de la dulce filomena
el soto y su donaire,
en la noche serena,
con llama que consume y no da
  pena.

The breathing of the air, The song of the sweet philomel, The grove and its beauty in the serene night, With a flame that consumes and gives no pain.

(Spiritual Canticle, Stanza XXXVIII)

"...the breathing of the air, which is the love whereof we have spoken... the song of the philomel, which is jubilation in praise of God... the serene night... pure and lofty contemplation... the flame that consumes and gives no pain...a flame of sweet transformation of love..." *(Spiritual Canticle,* Stanza XXXVIII, pp.175–176).

And again, "possessing as if not possessing": "Mine are the heavens and mine is the earth; mine are the people; the righteous are mine and mine are the sinners; the angels are mine and the Mother of God, and all things are mine; and God Himself is mine and for me, for Christ is mine and all for me. What, then, dost thou ask for and seek, my soul? *Thine is all this, and it is all for thee.* Despise not thyself nor give thou heed to the crumbs which fall from thy Father's table. Go thou forth and do thou glory in thy glory. Hide therein and rejoice and thou shalt have the desire of thy heart" (A Prayer of the Soul Enkindled with Love, *Maxims,* p. 244).

Eternal happiness.

"The tenth and last step of this secret ladder of love causes the soul to become wholly assimilated to God, by reason of the clear and immediate vision of God, which it then possesses; when, having ascended in this life to the ninth step, it goes forth from the flesh. These souls, who are few, enter not into purgatory, since they have already been wholly purged by love... *Beati mundo corde: quoniam ipsi Deum videbunt* (Matthew, 5:8) And...this vision is the cause of the perfect likeness of the soul to God, for, as S. John says, *we know that we shall be like Him* (I John, 3:2). Not because the soul will come to have the capacity of God, for that is impossible; but because all that it is will become like to God, *for which cause it will be called, and will be, God by participation...* But, on this last step of clear vision...there is naught that is hidden from the soul, by reason of its complete assimilation" *(Dark Night,* II, 20, p. 469–470).

CHAPTER IX

Conclusions

What can we add to these few pages? That man, "the apex of evolution
and revolutions," comes, rightly or wrongly, to perceive an infinite aspiration within himself. That he gives different, and sometimes irreconcilable,
explanations for this aspiration. That St. John of the Cross is a Christian,
in the Catholic tradition. That for Christians, as for Jews and for Moslems,
God is not only the "All," but the "Other" as well. That the Christian faith
is by no means accepted by all men of "good faith" and of "good will."
"Know thyself" counseled the oracle of Delphi. Without a doubt we know
ourselves (and we locate ourselves) a little better than the Greeks did, but
for many the night surrounding us is still dark. At any rate, no more for us
than for St. John of the Cross, existence, even that of God, does not result
from belief, nor does being from appearance.

BIBLIOGRAPHY

1. S. Weinberg: *The First Three Minutes: A Modern View of the Origin of the Universe.* Basic, New York, 1976.

2. Swâmi Nityabodhânanda, Ordre de Râmakrishna: *Actualité des Upanishads.* Maisonneuve et Larose, Paris, 1979.

3. R. Ardrey: *Hunting Hypothesis.* Atheneum, New York, 1976.

4. Y. Chesni: *Dialectical Realism. Towards a Philosophy of Growth.* Translated from the French by J. P. Zenk, The Live Oak Press, Palo Alto, 1987.

5. Ch. Darwin: *The Origin of Species.*

6. K. Lorenz, *On Aggression.* Translated by M. K. Wilson, Harcourt-Brace, San Diego, 1974.

7. André-Thomas, Y. Chesni, S. Saint-Anne Dargassies: *The Neurological Examination of the Infant.* Translated from the French and with a preface by R. C. MacKeith, P. E. Polani, E. Clayton-Jones, National Spastics Society & Heinemann, London, 1960. Out of print.

8. M. Blondel *in* A. Lalande: *Vocabulaire technique et critique de la philosophie.* Presses Universitaires de France, Paris, 1956 ("Mystique").

9. H. Bergson: *La pensée et le mouvant.* Presses Universitaires de France, Paris.

10. J. H. Jackson: *Selected Writings.* Hodder and Stoughton, London, 1931.

11. Y. Chesni: "Reflections concerning consciousness," in the present work.

12. I. Pavlov: *Selected Works.* Foreign Languages Publishing House, Moscow, 1955.

13. S. Freud: *The Future of an Illusion.* Edited by J. Strachey, Norton, New York, 1975.

14. Y. Chesni: "Psychoanalysis and freedom," in the present work.

15. Y. Battistini: *Trois présocratiques. Héraclite, Parménide, Empédocle.* Gallimard, Paris, 1968.

16. B. Russell: *History of Western Philosophy and its Connection with Political and Social Circumstances from the Earliest Times to the Present Day.* George Allen and Unwin, London, 1961.

17. Aristotle: *On the Soul.*

18. G. W. F. Hegel: *Preface to the Phenomenology of Spirit.*

19. J. Van Lawick-Goodall: *In the Shadow of Man.* Collins, St. James Place, London, 1970.

20. M. Eliade: *A History of Religious Ideas.* Three volumes, University of Chicago Press, Chicago, 1979–1988.

21. E. Freud: *Totem and Taboo.* Translated from the German by J. Strachey, Norton, New York, 1962.

22. E. O. James: *The Beginnings of Religion: An Introductory and Scientific Study.* Greenwood Press, New York, 1973.

23. *The Averbury Monuments.* Department of the Environment Official Handbook, London, 1976. *Stonehenge,* idem, 1977.

24. C. A. Newham: *The Astronomical Significance of Stonehenge.* Moon Publications, Shirenewton, Gwent, Wales, 1972.

25. S. N. Kramer: *History Begins at Sumer*. University of Pennsylvania Press, Philadelphia, 1981.

26. *Trésors du Musée de Bagdad*. Philipp von Zabern, Mainz, 1977.

27. E. Drioton, G. Contenau, J. Duchesne-Guillemin: *Religions of the Ancient East*. Hawthorn Books, New York, 1959.

28. J. Pirenne: *La Religion et la morale dans l'Egypte ancienne*. La Baconnière, Neuchâtel, 1965.

29. *Introductory Guide to the Egyptian Collections*. British Museum, London, 1971.

30. Aeschylus: *The Bacchantes*.

31. H. Jeanmaire: *Dionysios. Histoire du culte de Bacchus*. Payot, Paris, 1951.

32. Plato: *Complete Works*. Loeb Classical Library, Heinemann and Harvard University Press, London and Cambridge, Mass., 1961–1963.

33. E. Des Places: *La religion grecque. Dieux, cultes, rites et sentiment religieux dans la Grèce antique*. Picard, Paris, 1969.

34. Ch. Werner: *La Philosophie grecque*. Payot, Paris, 1946.

35. R. Schaerer: *Dieu, l'homme et la vie d'après Platon*. La Baconnière, Neuchâtel, 1944.

36. *The Orphic Hymns*. Translation from Greek into English by Apostolos N. Athanassakis, Scholars Press, Missoula, Montana, 1977.

37. T. A. Szlezak: *Platon und Aristoteles in der Nuslehre Plotins*. Schwabe, Basel-Stuttgart, 1979.

38. J. A. Cuttat: *La rencontre des religions, avec une étude sur la spiritualité de l'Orient chrétien*. Aubier, Paris, 1957.

39. Sa divine Grâce A. C. Bhaktivedanta Swâmi Prabhupâda, Acârya-fondateur de l'Association Internationale pour la Conscience de Krishna: *Le Srîmad Bhâgavatam*. Editions Bhâktivedanta, Paris, Luçay-le-Mâle, 36600 Valençay (Domaine d'Oublaisse), 1978.

40. M. Eliade: *Yoga: Immortality and Liberty*. Translated by R. Willard Trask, Princeton University Press, Princeton, 1970.

41. E. Jacobson: *Progressive Relaxation*. University of Chicago Press, Chicago, 1929. Midway Reprint, 1974.

42. F. J. McGuigan: *The Psychophysiology of Thinking. Studies of Covert Behavior*. Academic Press, New York, London, 1973.

43. Y. Chesni: "Consciousness and movement. Studies concerning the motor component of interior speech and visual imagination," in the present work.

44. Walpola Rahula: *What the Buddha Taught*. Grove Press, New York, 1974.

45. M. Eliade: *Shamanism: Archaic Techniques of Ecstacy*. Princeton University Press, Princeton, 1964.

46. *La mystique et les mystiques*. Desclée de Brouwer, 1965.

47. J. Ancelet-Hustache: *Maître Eckhart et la mystique rhénane*. Le Seuil, Paris, 1978.

48. F. Timmermans: *La harpe de saint François*. Bloud et Gay, Paris, 1961.

49. H. C. Puech: *En quête de la Gnose*. Gallimard, Paris, 1978.

50. *The New English Bible. With Apocrypha*. Oxford University Press, Cambridge University Press, 1970.

51. C. Journet: *The Meaning of Evil.* Translated from the French by Michael Barry, P. J. Kenedy, New York, 1963.

52. R. M. Mosse-Bastide: *Plotin.* Bordas, Paris, 1972.

53. S. Freud: *Moses and Monotheism.* Katherine Jones, editor, Random House, New York, 1955.

54. J. Maritain: *The Degrees of Knowledge.* Translated from the French by Gerald Phelan. Scribner, New York, 1959.

55. Pascal: *Pensées.*

56. J. Maritain: *Science et sagesse.* Labergerie, Paris.

57. *The Complete Works of Saint John of the Cross.* Edited and translated by E. Allison Peers. The Newman Bookshop, Westminster, Maryland, 1945.

58. J. G. Hondet, O.S.B., abbé de Belloc: *Les poèmes mystiques de saint Jean de la Croix.* Le Centurion, Paris, 1966.

59. E. Callot: *Les trois moments de la philosophie théologique de l'histoire. Augustin. Vico. Herder. Situation actuelle.* La Pensée Universelle, Paris, 1974.

PART FOUR

The Goals, Methods, and Limits of Psychotherapy*

*Conference given April 4, 1979 to the
Groupe Genevois de la Société Romande de Philosophie.

Psychotherapy, at first approximation, is the *treatment of the mind by the mind*. Within this vast subject I will limit myself to examining certain selected points, in reference to the three classic modalities of psychotherapy: analytical psychotherapy, relaxation psychotherapy and systematic desensitization, used separately or conjointly.

Psychotherapy deals chiefly with neuroses. After having reviewed what a *neurotic automatism* is—a repetitive, unconscious or barely conscious, involuntary behavior, the contrary of a free behavior—I will summarize the *methods* used by the three forms of psychotherapy for overcoming these obstacles. At the same time the *effects* and the *goals* of psychotherapy will begin to emerge: an aid in development, a freeing of the person.

I will then point out some of the connections that psychotherapy has with the theory of knowledge, the philosophy of nature, and ethics. I will be mindful of the facts that human being is a *unitary process,* whose corporeal and mental aspects do not exist independently of each other; that the knowledge of self and others is not "phenomenological," that it is neither a coincidence nor a separation nor filled with doubt, but a *relation* nuanced or potentially nuanced by different degrees of certitude; that development involves permanence and change, and that by nature it is *dialectical*. Through its methods and goals, psychotherapy will in turn emerge as profoundly *realistic* and *dialectical,* in accord with the deep sense of natural evolution, simply striving to remove obstacles to it. By definition psychotherapy is liberating. It has nothing to do with those illusory and ephemeral methods of mental coercion that sometimes seek to conceal themselves under the name of *psychiatry*.

In conclusion I will indicate three kinds of *limitations* for psychotherapy. Limitations in connection with "human nature" and particularly with the fact that a number of our genetic, hereditary, and innate virtualities are expressed in a relatively univocal fashion, and that their progressive actualization is in no way influenced by changes in the environment, including psychotherapy. Limitations of the moral order, depending on the professional ethics of the psychotherapist, his *Weltanschauung,* without forgetting that of his patient, to the extent that it is authentic. Limitations owing to the insufficiency of our technics or to that of the socio-economic and cultural conditions required for their employment.

CHAPTER X

Neurotic Automatisms

General characteristics of neurotic automatisms. Examples borrowed from the "Oedipus Complex."

I customarily explain to my patients that neurosis is the illness of *stoppage* and of *repetition*. Something becomes fixed in us during infancy and repeats itself indefinitely, while the rest of physical and mental growth takes place normally. It is these repetitions, the consequences of the fixation, that constitute neurotic automatisms.

That infantile something which is so pathologically fixed and repeated is a certain type of human relation. That relation, in its beginning, can in a certain way be adapted, and in that sense be logical and true. The inadaptation, the lack of logic and the error become increasingly manifest with the advance of age, as circumstances and the expected way of normal reacting change. A neurotic automatism is a kind of fossilized behavior.

Every little girl, for example, normally passes through the "Oedipal" stage, which is a triangular relation with two strong points, the father and mother, and one weak point, the child. The latter correctly resents the situation and, in sum, behaves accordingly. Desiring her father with a forbidden desire, hating the victorious rival in her mother while loving, needing her, and depending on her at the same time, she fears being punished by her. The worst of punishments would be the fulfillment of her conscious or unconscious wish that her mother go away or disappear, a fulfillment that would leave her finally alone with her father, but irremediably guilty and abandoned, a matricide.

When the child develops normally, these childish behaviors give way progressively to those of an adult. The resolution of the Oedipus Complex takes place partly through identification with the rival, i.e., with the parent of the same sex, then through "transcending" him or her. A new sexual object can be chosen and conquered, which is not simply a substitute for the parent who was formerly desired without hope. More optimistic bonds can be made with persons of the same sex. The character of the parents, the deliberate bestowing or withholding of their affective gifts, and in a general way the formative qualities of the surroundings contribute to that happy evolution.

On the contrary, under certain conditions and influences, infantile behavior becomes fixed. One important factor in fixation is an *inadequate environment*. This nevertheless does not mean that the unconscious, fixed parental *imagos* underlying the neurotic behavior constitute an exact re-collection of what the parents used to be. Even though she was neurotic, aggressive, subject to dreadful outbursts of anger, and used and abused corporal punishments, little Dennis' mother was never that gigantic *diplodocus* that ate him after he was transformed into a fly, which then devoured it from within. Even though they are often not devoid of some real foundation, these constructions are in great part subjective, illusory, phantasmic, and phantasmagorial.

Another factor in fixation is constituted through a particular *typology,* through a certain habitual way of reacting, whether this is acquired early or is constitutional and hereditary. The study of typologies, which goes back to the "temperaments" of Hippocrates, has been developed by the school of Pavlov, along with the study of conditional reflexes. For example, Pavlov showed that dogs with strong, inert temperaments were more readily subject to obsessional neuroses than others. In our species, that affection is like the "reverse side of the coin," like a morbid caricature of determination in goodness and the will for perfection, like a desire for the absolute which is deceived in its object...[1]

As for the parts played by the milieu and by heredity in neurotic behaviors, here as elsewhere it is often quite difficult to ascertain. The observation of univitellin twins can certainly help us. They, indeed, have an identical hereditary patrimony, while the conditions of their subsequent lives can differ.

In brief, neurotic automatisms are involuntary, coercive, unconscious, illogical, and unadapted repetitions. The repetition takes place not under the mode of identity, but under that of *analogy*. The same play is done endlessly, but with different actors, and these differences help to mask the profound identity of the drama, a factor of unconsciousness for the patient, and for the analyst one of the hardships of his calling. What is fixed, subsisting, and repetitious is a *structure* (e.g., the Oedipal structure). The psychotherapist must learn to think structurally, in order to be able to understand and help his patient to understand the illusory and apparently changing system of repetitive analogies that separates him from the world, from others, and from himself. The reason for the initial consultation is not usually the neurotic automatism as such, which the patient does not perceive at first, or whose deep meaning he fails to understand, but rather the pain, the obsessions, the inadequate emotions, a vague feeling of inadaptation or failure, an inability to be happy.

Oedipal neuroses. Pre-Oedipal neuroses. Mixed neuroses.

I have just made precisions in the notions of fixation, repetition, and neurotic automatism, while using the Oedipal structure as my prime example. The mechanisms of pre-Oedipal neuroses are the same, to such an extent that the earlier the fixations, the more archaic is the character of the repetitions. The illness develops before the triangular phase, in that of the dual relations between mother and child. At that time the so-called primary processes of thought predominate, such as displacement, substitution, symbolization, and analogy, which occur among animals as well,[2] in art, poetry, dreams, and at all stages of neuroses... It is the most primitive among them, *splitting, projection, introjection,* and *omnipotent defense,* that will give pre-Oedipal neuroses a nuance so special that certain psychiatrists qualify them (wrongly, in my opinion) as "psychoses," confusing them with mental illnesses that include those of an entirely different nature (hereditary, toxic, etc.).

Splitting is the impossibility of conceiving an object, previously shown as having a white side and a black side, in a manner other than as two entirely different objects when viewed first on the one side and then on the other. Affectively, it is the radical separation between hate and love.[3]

Splitting betrays a *difficulty with synthesis,* normal with the very young child and animals, but abnormally persisting among neurotics. It is likewise in accord with what Freud called "the outward deflection of the death wish." What is initially split, as a matter of fact, is the Ego or what takes its place: all love at some times, all hate at others. For the nursling, now plunged into the beatitude of the breast, and then, due to whatever frustration, overtaken by absolutely total rage, there are two mothers, two bosoms: one completely delightful, paradise; the other completely frustrating and detestable, hell. Like the instinctual animal, it is ruled by a sign and fails to understand the whole. At the same time it projects its split affects onto the object, attributing to it the feelings it is experiencing in regard to it. To be sure, the splitting, changing character of a partner can provoke or facilitate those of the other, but parental *imagos* are often very different from real parents, notably as a result of projection. The persecuted persecutors and devoured devourers are retarded infants at the breast in the adult: such was that thirty year old patient, held prey by oral phantasies, who sometimes imagined himself to be a scorpion running rampant through the veins of his victims, feeding upon their blood and finally poisoned by their brains; such was little Dennis, transformed into a fly, devouring the entrails of the diplodocus that had swallowed him...

It is with this "diplodocus child" that I wish to detain you a bit longer, to illustrate another primary thought process susceptible of persisting pathologically in the adult: *defense through omnipotence*. When his imaginary friends, the lions and the apes, were insufficient to defend him against his terrible adversaries, the child would change himself into an all powerful magician. With a stroke of his wand he would reduce his enemies to the size of an inoffensive mouse, or make them disappear. From time to time, through inadvertence or, later, through increased insight, he would forget to substitute others for his parents and would annihilate the latter; but, otherwise a loving son, he hastened to revive them... One day this young wonder-worker confided in me that, in order to fight against such powerful enemies (who he did not yet realize were in part only the illusory projection of his own aggressivity), he needed to be God, and even "more than God!" Perhaps we should see here one of the roots of the strange human desire to become divine...[4]

If circumstances allow it—exterior circumstances, subsequently interiorized and recast—anatomical and functional maturation manifests itself by the increase of synthesis. After the *schizoid* phase, characterized by the predominance of splitting, there follows the "depressive" stage, in which aggressivity is mingled with love and therefore repentance. In passing, note that the Kleinian nomenclature contains an asymmetry: the word "schizoid" indeed describes well the splitting (at the risk, moreover, of a confusion with schizophrenia), while that of "depression" refers to a consequence of diminished splitting, to an increased synthesis: regret in having done evil, or having wished to do evil, to a person who is henceforth looked upon as a unity that simply has good and less good aspects. This in no way reduces the value of Klein's analysis of early, normal, stages of human development, and of their neurotic fixations.

Neuroses are frequently mixed, with Oedipal and pre-Oedipal elements. Shakespeare, who knew well the human soul, has described a tragic, mixed neurosis in Othello:

And let the labouring bark climb hills of seas
Olympus-high, and duck again as low
As hell's from heaven!

Such is the life of Othello, now at the zenith of the sea's billows, now at their nadir. This is what will repeat itself one more time, the last, with his unhappy wife. Desdemona has a weakness for Cassio, who is of the same race as she. Iago, Othello's evil Ego, fans the flame. Frustrated Oedipal love, real or imaginary, provokes in Othello a pre-Oedipal regression, the splitting of the object, murder, and suicide. Desdemona, the "pure source of his life," became "a cistern for foul toads to knot and gender in." A mixed image, at once Oedipal and split, with apportionment, the superposition of substituted images, and the contemptuous and reassuring reducing of enemies...

Oedipal, pre-Oedipal, or mixed, neurotic automatisms connote a lack in the development of consciousness, and, with it, of reason, will, and freedom. Like the instinctive animal and the small child, neurotics are incapable of understanding the whole, of placing the parts in relation to each other and to the whole. They react blindly, involuntarily, to signs out of context. They split reality. They see in it nothing except that to which they are sensitized. What is interrupted is the development of the analytic-synthetic dialectic, one of the major modalities of normal growth.[5]

The objective of psychotherapy is to unlock this development and to accelerate it, to restart the passage of time and to recapture lost time. Under its influence, when the treatment is successful, one can observe a kind of abridged development of the human person.

CHAPTER XI

Technics and Effects of Analytical Psychotherapy, Progressive Relaxation, Systematic Desensitization, and Synthetic Approaches

Analytical psychotherapy.

Analytical psychotherapy attempts to treat psychological illnesses, particularly neuroses, by psychological means, the *grasp of consciousness*, or *insight*, and the *modification of the relation between the patient and the psychotherapist.*[6]

The grasp of consciousness takes place through the analysis of the associations of spontaneous ideas, dreams, and especially of transference, i.e., of neurotic repetition in the therapeutic relationship, a present more easily accessible than a distant past, repressed or even dating from a time when the cerebral and functional development of the child was insufficient to form mnemonic traces, whether visual or verbal. It bears on the neurotic repetition and its basic meaning, i.e., its analogy with behaviors dating from childhood. When, for one reason or another, the latter are unable to be remembered, what is proposed to the patient is a prudent *reconstruc-*

tion of his distant past, i.e., the most probable extrapolation, backwards, of the data that can be gathered in the course of analysis. In each case— the analysis of the association of ideas, of dreams, or of transference—the psychoanalyst, at each instant, should find a reasonable compromise, which is often difficult, between the need to listen, observe, and remain silent, and that of prudently communicating to the patient prudent *interpretations.* Another difficulty is the persistence of the forces of repression, those very same that previously had transformed a part of the life of the child into isolated pathogenic sectors: they hardly become conscious when they are repressed anew and forgotten. Another, the analogical feature of neurotic repetitions, with the substitutions of characters and situations in which the analogies can continue to mask the similarities for a long time. Another, the secondary benefits of neuroses... But these difficulties are not insurmountable, and furthermore, as I will be discussing, we now have other means at our disposal for bringing about a successful and rapid end to an interminable psychoanalysis.

When the grasp of consciousness has become deep and lasting, the neurotic automatism, unconscious by nature, disappears. The therapeutic relation and with it, analogically, the entirety of human relationships are freed little by little from the neurotic transference. There is an increase in consciousness, reason, will, freedom, and Ego growth in the realm of its greatest authenticity.

Progressive relaxation.

The human being can be known under exterior aspects—anatomophysiological and behavioral—and interior, mental aspects, either engaging in self-introspection or inferring in others a consciousness analogous to one's own, based on the analogy of directly observable exterior aspects. Neither man's body nor his spirit have separate existences of their own. A number of psychoanalysts have no doubt about that, even though psychoanalysis has to do principally with consciousness and that which is unconscious initially but can and should become conscious. Inversely, neither progressive relaxation nor systematic desensitization are exclusively corporal and behavioral approaches. Like psychoanalysis, both aim at curing the man, body and soul. Both appeal constantly to the introspection of the patient, even though in ways that differ from each other in part and from psychoanalysis. Let us start with progressive relaxation, discovered by the American master Edmund Jacobson in the first half of the century, about the same time that the Austrian Schultz discovered "autogeneous training."

Even when we are apparently immobile, a large part of our activity, though it is as interior as thinking and certain emotions, in reality contains a hint of movement. A number of philosophers and psychologists used to suppose this, without experimental proof, men such as Ribot, James, Bergson, and Piaget.[7] Electromyography, relaxation, as well as indirect proofs, have largely confirmed these views.[8, 9, 10] The effect of relaxation is double: the suppression of emotional and ideational automatisms through the suppression of their tensional, neuro-motor aspect; and the setting at rest of the whole of the nervous system through the suppression of the general excitation provoked in it by the centripetal influxes originating from muscles under tension (diffusion of the excitation). It is the second mechanism that intervenes in the treatment of functional troubles of the smooth musculature, such as that of the digestive track, blood vessels, etc., which is mostly or completely beyond the control of the will, and therefore mostly or completely inaccessible to relaxation *directly*.

Relaxation according to Jacobson involves a double progression: a spatial progression, muscle group by muscle group; and a progression in depth. Because it constantly calls upon the introspection of the subject, the method presents itself explicitly as "non behavioral." Nor is it more psychoanalytical, since the introspection bears only on feelings in the muscle system. It excludes the hypnotic procedures of autogeneous training. It is based upon the education of muscular feeling, the primary condition of relaxation. The use of artificial biofeedback (the transformation of action currents in the muscles into signals perceptible by other sense organs) is not forbidden, but it is not recommended in principle: for the point is to teach the patient in all circumstances to perceive directly the tensions in his muscles. Electronic equipment can be used to measure the tension level and the progress in relaxation. These can also be ascertained clinically by the degree of resistance to passive mobilization, the respiratory rhythm, and the intensity of the kneecap reflex. When the fingers are placed lightly on closed eyelids they detect the movements of the eyeballs during visual thinking and the cessation of these movements during the relaxation of the eye muscles and the extinction of images. We have no simple means at our disposal for appreciating the tension level of the speech muscles, i.e., the neuro-motor aspect of verbal thought.

The cure takes place in two phases: general relaxation, with the patient closing his eyes and reclining, and relaxation during normal activity, or "differential" relaxation. In this second phase the patient learns to distinguish between useful and useless activity, i.e., to utilize only that energy which is necessary and sufficient for the task at hand, and to eliminate parasitical tensions, emotions, and thoughts. Often I achieve the cure through a systematic desensitization based on relaxation, another form of psychotherapy to which I will return. The duration of the treatment is a few months, and that constitutes another difference from psychoanalysis. Nevertheless, if the technic of relaxing can be taught fairly rapidly, its voluntary, conscious practice should continue much longer, to the point where the relaxed behavior becomes a new habit. If choice of treatment has been adequate, the cure conducted correctly, and the patient intelligent, cooperative, and gifted with sufficient determination, the results are generally good, and very probably superior to those obtainable through simple human contact, independently of the method used.

To be sure, a number of our higher processes, including even the most interior of these, necessarily contains a hint of movement. Nevertheless, we ought to avoid excessive generalization. Among patients suffering from mental slowness along with associated peripheral neuro-motor trouble, sense activities occur with normal delays.[10] In motor aphasia, verbal comprehension is not suppressed. In deep relaxation, the instructor continues to be understood. When all active thought has been suppressed, one can have the experience as it were of a total receptivity and openness, of a limitless dilation. Let us recall that it is by means of an analogous *passivity,* through the extinguishing of our petty, limiting activities which lack proportion, that mystics in both the East and the West arrive at what they believe to be the love union with God, divinization by nature or by participation, or undifferentiated fusion within the All.[4]

Edmund Jacobson insists on the fact that progressive relaxation is not a "behavioral therapy," but a treatment of the human spirit—the human mind—by means other than pharmacological, based on the introspection of muscular feelings, and on a human relationship, the one between the subject of relaxation and its director. It is really a *psychotherapy,* even though quite different from psychoanalysis. Nevertheless, in reference to systematic desensitization and synthetic approaches, we will see that, in relaxation, introspection and the act of consciousness can go beyond muscular feeling and the human relationship between the teacher and the taught, and that there is no necessary *hiatus* or opposition between the three kinds of psychotherapy.

Systematic desensitization.

"Systematic desensitization results in deconditioning anxiety by counter-posing the anxiety-inhibiting effects of relaxation to weak evocations of anxiety."[11]

Systematic desensitization, an off-shoot of behavioral therapy (and in many ways going beyond it), seeks to suppress anxiety, which it considers the essential component of a number of mental or psychosomatic affec-tions, and really nothing more than a defective conditioning, a bad habit. It is relaxation which is used as a means of deconditioning.

After a simplified and accelerated course on relaxation, the cure pro-ceeds by relaxing while the imagination dwells on anxiety laden situa-tions. These latter have been previously classified into groups as natural as possible, preference being given to structure types; I will return shortly to these last two notions. If the indications have been correctly posed, the analysis, grouping, ranking, and choice of anxiety laden situations done well, if the therapist has mastered the technic sufficiently and the sub-ject's capacities are adequate, experience shows that the anxiety diminish-es with each repetition and that, when it is finally suppressed in the imag-ined situation, this result is transferred to the real situation.

The mechanism of desensitization is subject to discussion. Wolpe is of the opinion that it is a matter of an authentic Pavlovian deconditioning. It is also possible to consider the treatment as consisting in interiorized trials with progressive correction of errors. The interiorization of trials consti-tutes one of the greatest marks of progress for intelligence, and it is not impossible that there has been something of an analog on the affective plane. Satisfaction, the well being accompanying relaxation, probably also plays a role, and likewise the reassuring presence of the psychotherapist. But here again, the proportion of favorable results clearly appears higher than what can be obtained by simple human contact with no particular technic.

How can desensitization, using only current anxiety laden situations, known to the patient, cure a neurosis, where the pathological fixations derive from infancy, where the situations that trigger the neurotic automatism constantly substitute for each other, where the successive *characters* are but masks that mask other masks, which conceal deformed parental *imagos* from the past, where differences hide identities, where the process as a whole is fundamentally unconscious and remains so in the absence of psychoanalysis? When (as, it seems, there is frequently the case) desensitization is radically curative, i.e., excludes all new substitution symptoms, the explanation could be the following: what has been eliminated are pathological *structures* that are not only *common* to the current anxiety laden situations, but also to past situations, forgotten by the patient, as well as to all possible analogous situations, i.e., those which might be able to occur in the future.

Is systematic desensitization a "behavioral therapy?" Not if, with its founder Watson, the latter pretends to exclude consciousness from its investigation, under the pretext that consciousness, being subjective, would be unsuitable as an object of scientific knowledge. Systematic desensitization, indeed, makes constant appeal to the introspection of the patient: in the definition of anxiety laden situations; in relaxation based on muscular feeling; in communicating the degree and location of muscular tensions.* But *neo-behaviorism,* though still refusing to take account of the Freudian unconscious, assigns an increasingly large place to consciousness. It therefore has no difficulty in embracing systematic desensitization as a *psychotherapy.*

Synthetic approaches.

Far from being opposed, analytical psychotherapy, progressive relaxation, and systematic desensitization are capable of helping each other. The approach is consequently synthetic. As in any synthesis, certain component characteristics can disappear and certain new properties can appear. One of these new properties could be the *rapidity* of effective treatment.

The relative brevity of desensitization treatment is probably related to its synthetic character. The relaxation instruction is abridged; the imagining of anxiety laden situations and the communicating of the degrees of

---

*Bergson has reminded us that consciousness is not quantifiable.[7] With this reservation, the "anxiety scale," coded from zero to a hundred, which Wolpe uses in systematic desensitization, remains for the patient a convenient means of briefly communicating the qualitative changes of the flow of his consciousness to the therapist.

anxiety maintain eye and voice muscle activity; the patient points to the place where he is feeling tension. Nevertheless I personally insist a little more than Wolpe on the teaching of relaxation and, in the course of desensitization, I ask my patients to relax still more deeply, without imagining or communicating, immediately before and after each exercise.

Progressive relaxation and systematic desensitization can help end those interminable psychoanalyses in which, after initial progress, a kind of stagnation manifests itself in relation to the persistence of the forces of repression, resistance, an overly strong anxiety or inhibition, an inaptitude to follow the fundamental rule of saying all, quasi bodily habits, the secondary advantages of the neurosis, an unshakable dependency, etc.[12] Coming after an analytical cure, desensitization is facilitated by insight, by a certain conscious grasping of the neurotic automatisms, of their meaning, their history. The grouping of the anxiety laden situations is rendered easier, clearer, more natural. The neurotic reactions have already diminished in intensity.[13]

Inversely, when by themselves alone they have not been sufficient, progressive relaxation and systematic desensitization can constitute an excellent introduction to an analytical therapy which, without them, may have been impossible or more difficult, longer, less fruitful.

In my opinion, desensitization should be tried first, or when simple relaxation is slow in mastering the anxiety laden situations. If this is necessary, the relaxation will be completed in due course, it will be possible to return to desensitization, and the analytical method will still be in reserve. The use of medication, whether as an exclusive treatment or as a support for psychotherapy, exceeds the limits of this study.

CHAPTER XII

Philosophical Points of View

The unity of man. Realism of knowledge. The notions of aspects and relation.

Human reality is a unitary process, knowable through *interior* , i.e., conscious aspects, and under *exterior,* anatomophysiological and behavioral aspects.[5] One's proper consciousness is known by means of introspection, and that of the other by inference: from the analogy of exterior aspects, and particularly from verbal accounts that the other can make of his introspection, we infer an analogy between his interior aspects and our own.

To know is neither to coincide nor to be separate. It is to be in *relation.* The notion of aspects connotes the various modalities of this relation. Even when, through introspection, one knows his own consciousness, no matter how much he studies it and reflects on it, he still does not coincide with it; between his spontaneous consciousness and reflection on it, there is a difference of precisely one degree of reflection. Knowing, moreover, is not being separated. Phenomenology is mistaken in pretending to reduce the philosopher's knowing to the description of his states of consciousness, to an "egology," by placing between parentheses as doubtful the existence of all that is not his consciousness and which ends up by disappearing in its own turn, like everything else, in the obsessional reduction. The "apodictic, certain, and present evidence," outside of which nothing would be sure, is the phenomenological "peau de chagrin" which, according to Balzac, constantly diminishes and finally disappears. Sartre and Heidegger bear witness to this: in the end they found themselves stripped of phenomenology itself and were obliged, as the saying goes, to begin again from zero. As for the notion of relation, it does not include that of a necessary confusion between the two terms of the relation, the reality capable of being known and the subject that can know, whose common act constitutes knowledge.[14] Another trap is the *hypostasizing* of our conscious aspect, providing it with the illusion of an independent existence through ignorance of our anatomophysiological aspects. This ignorance can result from a general lack of development among the sciences, an excess of specialization, or other reasons. An inverse error consists in making consciousness an epiphenomenon of the brain's activity.[5]

The psychotherapist does not doubt the existence of his patient. He does not feel irremediably cut off from him. He infers in him a consciousness analogous to his own. The psychoanalyst is interested in this fringe of consciousness capable of being communicated in words and which provides access to the unconscious; he ignores the feelings of muscular tension. It is principally these that the relaxation therapist takes into account. The behavioral therapist, when he practices desensitization, adds anxiety and anxiety laden situations.

The psychotherapist, not, like the phenomenologists, doubting the existence of his object—the patient—, and not, like the Kantian idealists, believing that he and his patient are radically separated from each other by the *a priori* categories and forms of sensibility and intelligence, alters him throughout the course of the cure, which is precisely the goal. Are we then in the presence of a particular case of *confusionism,* where knowable reality and the knowing subject are indeed the two terms of the knowledge relation, but where their respective parts would be impossible to distinguish, first of all because in that relation, even disregarding counter transference, the first term is really and constantly modified by the second? This is the same pretended impossibility, grounded in the same pretended insurmountable obstacle, upon which the idealist microphysicists build their argument: the microphysical x would be unknowable because it is modified necessarily by the methods set in motion to study it: it would be impossible ever to know anything except an inescapable mix of observer and observed. I have spoken elsewhere about what ought to be thought about confusionism in general and microphysical confusionism in particular.[5, 14] As far as psychotherapy is concerned, the difficulty to which I just alluded does not exist. To be sure, the goal of psychotherapy is to free the patient of his tensions, his anxieties, his neurotic automatisms. And the cured patient is indeed different from what he was before the cure. But it is no less true that the past remains what it has been, that the tensions, anxieties, and neurotic reactions were able to be observed, noted, and recorded at the beginning of the cure and were attenuated only slowly during its course. The psychotherapist, the psychoanalyst, and soon the patient as well, become capable of remembering the *history* of the illness, even though that history was affected by the treatment.

Relaxation and desensitization are able to grasp the patient under his exterior and interior aspects. Though Freud, a physician, trained as a neurologist, was very interested in the mind, he was by no means ignorant of the body; he foresaw, along with others, the importance of hormones among the sources of the drives. The same cannot be said for all of his successors, one group of whom literally hypostasized Freud's psychic apparatus and forgot the body. For proof of which I offer the transfer (a disastrous one, in my opinion) of psychoanalysis to the sections of psychology within faculties of letters.

The direction of evolution. Its dialectical character. The meaning and limits of psychotherapy.

When viewed broadly enough, in a sufficient scale of time, biological evolution shows a progressive lessening of control by signs isolated from context, and an increase in the faculty of understanding wholes, of situating parts in their relations to each other and to the whole, and of behaving accordingly. There in the history of species, of societies and individuals, in that of the human Ego, is the rising road that leads from innate reflexes, rigidly preadapted by the anterior development of species, to an intelligence that does not suppress the instincts but clarifies them as well as the examples, prescriptions, interdictions, silences, and taboos of the group.

Among different or contrary movements, whose struggle can itself be a cause for progress, the perfecting of analysis and synthesis, the progressive grasp of consciousness of the whole within the part, of the universe within man, even God, as believers think, through His human image, mark the profound, permanent direction of change. Evolution takes place within relation, through relation, and for relation between real originalities in the heart of the "organic unity of the whole."[15] It is, in that sense, *dialectical*. Under certain conditions, the analytico-synthetic dialectic and the conflict dialectic mutually support each other, as when combat sharpens intelligence and intelligence favors the victory of the fittest and the sublimation of combat.[5]

Psychotherapy does not try to modify the profound direction of evolution. It would be incapable of doing so. It simply strives to clear away some of the interior obstacles which oppose the blossoming of man. To borrow an image from Pascal, it is situated between two infinities: that of our ignorance, our foolishness, our weakness, the difficulty we have in mastering our old instincts, our ability to disguise them under the appearances of reason, our capacity for unconsciousness, —and that of our possibilities for spiritual growth. It is, by definition, the contrary of those totalitarian or otherwise interested endeavors whose hidden or avowed object is to induce acceptance, by means of psychological pressures, through the fallacious pretext of social adaptation, of unacceptable situations, to maintain a certain *status quo*, and to block any true development.

Different nuances, however, can probably be discerned in the objectives and results of various psychotherapies. The Freudian Ego, developed and reinforced by psychoanalysis, has something active about it, not to say activist. Jacobson's Ego, at least in extreme relaxation, is disencumbered of any surface agitation which prevents it from reflecting the depths of reality. More so than Freud's Ego, it is "naked and empty"—*desnudez y vacio,* as St. John of the Cross put it—, passive, *open.* A distant relative of yoga, or the result of a parallel evolution, progressive relaxation is *purgative* in the mystical sense of the word.[16, 4]

The phenotype, i.e., the realized living being, is a function of genetic patrimony and the environment. In the course of development certain genetic virtualities unfold in relative independence from the milieu, while others are more sensitive to it: cultivated in ordinary soil or in slate soil, an hydrangea will have the same general morphology; but in the first case its flowers are red, and in the second blue. In the present state of science, man is not moldable at will. This is the case for both heredity—directed selection, genetic surgery, etc.—and milieu—socio-economic and cultural conditions, education, upbringing, training, conditioning... These *genetic limitations,* however, are no more in contradiction to a certain functional unlimitation than, for example, the anatomy of a musical instrument to the infinity of melodies that one can draw from it. The violin, nevertheless, is superior to the viol and the piano to the harpsichord.

From the previous evolution of species, from the past's vital confrontation, we have inherited our instincts. These are not reducible to sexuality and aggression, the two re-discoveries of psychoanalysis. Ethology has added the *instincts* towards territory, hierarchy, service, cleanliness, play, exploration for the sake of exploration, a kind of disinterested concern for beings... We are far from having made a complete inventory of them in our own species, primarily because, being reasoning animals, we have a tendency to believe that we reason more than animals do. And still these instincts are a part of us, as inescapably as any other important biological function like eating or breathing. Psychotherapy cannot make men into purely rational, disincarnated creatures, nor abandon them to their old unchained instincts in a way that brute beasts themselves would not know. It tries, as I said, to strengthen the Ego, to free it from the shackles of neurosis, to allow it not to suppress our instincts, nor to serve them unconditionally, but to master, impound, channel, and use them for more human ends.

Often enough, unfortunately, the use of psychotherapy is limited by the *socio-economic* and *cultural* situation. A moment ago I called to mind the mental constraints that some here and there attempt to force on everyone, even to the point of trying lead psychiatry astray for their profit. But, far more to the point, how do you pretend to help humanity in its development when two thirds of it is dying of hunger? How does one bring the priceless moral aid of a psychotherapy to the poor who would have need of it, but who are without the means and whom no one is able or willing to help? How, on the contrary, can we refuse the participation of social organisms in treatment under the fallacious pretext of "purifying the monetary relation," thus transforming psychoanalysis into a class therapy? How do you bring the ignorant "righteous" to understand that a neurosis is not a vice, nor a sin, that exaggerating guilt often does no more than aggravate things, that exhortations, confessions, penances, absolutions, good resolutions and prayers usually lead to nothing and that Freud is not the devil? How do you help a genetically healthy individual who is irremediably deformed by his milieu, prevented, or simply discouraged by it from being treated? The list of exterior obstacles to psychotherapy and more generally to a kind of human liberation, could go on indefinitely. In my opinion, these obstacles will end up by being swept away by the irresistible torrent of evolution.

What our patients are first aware of, what they complain about, what they want to be delivered from, is the anxiety, the obsessions, phobias, impulses, psychosomatic disturbances, a vague sense of inadaptation and failure. In attempting to offer them relief, we give them as well the advantage of a little increase in freedom, and, with it, a little more true happiness.

BIBLIOGRAPHY

1. Y. Chesni: "Quelques problèmes à propos de la névrose obsessionelle." Archives Suisses de Neurologie, Neurochirugie et Psychiatrie, *103*, 2, 1969, 428–432.

2. K. Lorenz: *Studies in Animal and Human Behaviour.* Translated from the German by Robert Martin, Harvard University Press, Cambridge, 1970–71.

3. M. Klein and J. Riviere: *Love, Guilt, Reparation.* DeLacorte, New York, 1976.

4. Y. Chesni: "A tentative interpretation of St. John of the Cross within natural, open perspectives," in the present work.

5. Y. Chesni: *Dialectical Realism. Towards a Philosophy of Growth.* Translated from the French by J. P. Zenk, Palo Alto, The Live Oak Press, 1987.

6. S. Freud: *The Complete Psychological Works.* Standard Edition. Norton, New York, 1976.

7. H. Bergson: *Time and Free Will: An Essay on the Immediate Data of Consciousness.* Humanities Press, New York, 1971.

8. E. Jacobson: *Progressive Relaxation.* University of Chicago Press, Chicago, 1929; Midway Reprint, 1974.

9. F. J. McGuigan and R. A. Schoonover: *The Psychophysiology of Thinking. Studies of Covert Processes.* Academic Press, New York and London, 1973.

10. Y. Chesni: "Consciousness and movement. Studies concerning the motor component of interior speech and visual imagination," in the present work.

11. J. Wolpe: *The Practice of Behavior Therapy.* Pergamon, Elmsford, 1982.

12. S. Freud: *Analysis Terminable and Interminable. The Complete Psychological Works.* Standard Edition. Norton, New York, 1976.

13. Y. Chesni: "A Happy Conclusion of a Psychoanalytical Psychotherapy by Progressive Relaxation and Systematic Desensitization. Note on Synthetic Approach" Communication given at the First AAATC International, Interdisciplinary Conference on Stress and Tension Control, London, 1979, Plenum Press, New York and London, 1980, 157–162.

14. Y. Chesni: "Reflections concerning Consciousness," in the present work.

15. G.-W.-F. Hegel: *Phenomenology of Spirit.* Oxford University Press, New York, 1977.

16. M. Eliade: *Yoga: Immortality and Liberty.* Translated by R. Willard Trask, Princeton University Press, Princeton, 1970.

PART FIVE

Consciousness and Movement

Studies Concerning the Motor Component of Inner Speech and Visual Imagination*

*Dinner Address at the fourth annual reunion
of the American Association for the
Advancement of Tension Control,
introduced by E. Jacobson, Chicago, October, 1977
(Proceedings of the Fourth Annual Meeting of the
AAATC, McGuigan, Louisville, Kentucky, 1977).
The non-specialized reader may choose to read the
beginning and the end only.

Thought is an *interiorized action,* mimicking the past and sketching out the future through imagined, minuscule, covert movements which allow reversible mental operations. This is one of the main themes of leading modern psychologists, such as James, Ribot, Bergson,[1] Piaget,[2, 3] and many others. The inner word is a proprioceptive sign, according to Pavlov.[4] But the merit goes to Edmund Jacobson for being the first to have experimentally and systematically shown that internalization is frequently incomplete by demonstrating the existence of muscular action potentials during many mental processes, and the simultaneous diminution or suppression of both muscular and mental activities during relaxation.[5, 6, 7, 8, 9] Let me cite the American master: "The mind is that function of the animal organism which programs its conduct... We have need for abridged, abbreviated action-patterns, thus furnished by our musculature. By this means man represents to himself past experiences in recall and future experiences on a test-trial basis... It has been shown in our laboratory that tension is really part and parcel of what we commonly call the 'mind' (even if we do not realize it). The patterns in our muscles vary from moment to moment, constituting in part the *modus operandi* of our thinking. These patterns are minuscule and engage muscles variously all over the body, just as our grossly visible movements do."[7]

Jacobson's discoveries were the departure point for theoretical and practical research of the highest interest, in a wide range of fields, throughout the entire world. In the United States, Professor McGuigan and his staff are studying covert behavior.[10, 11, 12] In the U.S.S.R., Sokolov is working along the same lines.[13] Scientists have increasingly sophisticated means at their disposal: electromyography, electroencephalography, the recording of potentials in single neurones, etc. At the 11th World Congress of Neurology in Amsterdam we were presented with amazing slides showing in color the different levels of cerebral blood flow correlated with nervous activity; the normal subject at rest, with no apparent movement, exhibits moderate activity in most of the brain's motor areas; this activity is diminished with "schizophrenic" patients who have poor contact and ideation; very small areas light up during localized movements.[14]

I have a double purpose in coming to Chicago and taking part in the meeting of the American Association for the Advancement of Tension Control. First, to improve my knowledge in this new field that offers such promise for neurology, psychiatry, and psychotherapy. On this subject, allow me to bring to your attention a little statistical research in the field carried out on my Geneva patients suffering from neuropsychiatrical disorders: 88% of them had symptoms of tetany! Magnesium clearly can help in these cases, particularly since there is probably a general lack of magnesium in the diets of our western populations; but it is not a panacea.[15] My second purpose is to respond to the honor that Professors Jacobson and McGuigan extended to me when they asked me to present you with some of my research concerning the motor component of inner speech and visual imagination, or at least of some forms of these mental processes.

Along with some basic works, I will refer mainly to my own publications. Readers will find other bibliographical references in these books and articles. A necessary addition to these is Professor Wolpe's outstanding treatment by systematic desensitization, which is based on progressive relaxation but goes beyond it.[35]

A psychophysiological method based on the measure of time.

It is possible to express the psychophysio-physical relation in the form of a mathematical *function*. This function must contain only homogeneous terms, which belong respectively to the physical stimulus and to both the mental and the anatomophysiological aspects of the subject under study. *Time,* measured by a clock, figures among these common elements: moments, coinciding or not; lines of succession; intervals of time, etc.[16] From the anatomophysiological point of view, the interval of time between the stimulus and the beginning of the corresponding mental modification represents the sum of times of neurone excitation, dendritic and axonal conduction, and the crossing of synapses. The method used here in the study of our higher activity is the same as that which is currently used today in electrophysiological laboratories to evaluate peripheral nervous conduction.

After an *ad hoc* visual stimulation the hand show indicating a simple sensation takes place on an average of between the 150th and 250th millisecond; that of the *gnosia* (the non-verbal recognition of the object presented) between the 250th and 300th millisecond; and the microphonic recording of the word begins between the 550th and 600th millisecond.[17j,l,w] From the anatomophysiological point of view, this succession of moments, these increasing intervals of time, correspond to the activity of nerve areas more and more distant from the sensory organ and more and more complex, to which are added either the cerebral-manual or the cerebral-vocal signalling time.

It is possible to study other psychophysio-physical times in the same way: for instance the hand signal indicating the perception of a simple noise, distributed under certain conditions, requires about 200 milliseconds, and about 570 milliseconds are needed for a word to evoke a visual image and the latter to be indicated by a gesture. The cerebral-manual time is the same in both experiments, so the difference between the two total times, about 370 milliseconds, represents from the anatomophysio-physical point of view the time necessary for exciting the higher nerve structures relating to verbal comprehension and visual imagination.*[17j]

For purposes of comparison, remember that the different elements of the electroretinogram appear between 5 and 50 milliseconds after visual stimulation, and those of the electrocorticogram between 15 and 100 milliseconds. In 1954, Lilly and Cherry showed that the propagation speed of nervous activity in the auditory cortex of a cat is about 10 centimeters per second.[19] This corresponds approximately with our own results, even though a cat's brain is simpler than ours.

Repetition accelerates the processes to a certain extent. The French word "coq," repeated three times randomly interspersed among other words, triggers hand signals that the image of a rooster has appeared successively after 950, 600, and 450 milliseconds. It is possible that this is partly or totally due to what physiologists call a synaptic facilitation. The acceleration of certain performances through repetition is sometimes spectacular in patients who previously suffered from a pathological slowing of these performances. For instance, in one of my patients suffering from *amnestic-aphasia,* the time taken for non-verbal recognition (gnosia) was approximately normal, although naming the object was either impossible or considerably delayed (as much as several seconds). Repeating the same test, with different objects interspersed, rapidly led to a near normalization of the naming time, which lasted for several days. The facilitation curve had an exponential look.[17j, n] E. Weigl, with his *Arbeitsgruppe für Sprachpathologie,* made similar observations ("temporary deblocking in aphasia"[20, 21]), and Kreindler also points out these facilitation processes.[22]

---

*In this flashing succession of moments, proceeding in a few hundredths of a second from unconscious reflexes and raw sensation all the way to the most sophisticated forms of intelligence, is contained the whole of biological evolution: that of the subject—a few dozen years—and that of species—three or three and a half billion years.

The slowing of both outer and inner speech resulting from a disorder affecting different levels in the neuro-motor pathways below the classical areas of language in the brain. Similar observations regarding visual imagination.

In the course of about fifteen years of research I was able to show a slowing of both inner and outer speech, in approximately the same proportions, in a number of patients suffering from neurological disorders at different levels of the corticospinal pathway, from the precentral gyrus to the lower, bulbar motor neurone, and of the extrapyramidal structures and cerebellum. I also examined patients after laryngectomy. I was able to explain the apparent exception constituted by stammering, where outer speech is much more difficult than inner. Here again I will limit myself to giving a few clinical examples and some data. But I would like to make it clear that both the beginning and ending of inner speech are indicated by the patient's hand signals, and that the possible difficulties in the hand signals tend to cancel each other.

A young woman with normal intelligence and no true aphasia suffered from major dysarthria following two successive strokes involving both precentral gyri *("opercules rolandiques")*, most probably due to a vascular obstruction, predominately motor *("diplégie facio-linguo-masticatrice"[23])*. Her inner and outer speech, in about the same proportions, were three or four times slower than in a normal subject.[17q]

A young man of thirty with normal intelligence and no symptoms of aphasia was suffering from *Little's disease,* with extrapyramidal components (both choreic and athetoid movements), and had undergone an operation on the cervical spinal nerve roots and on the left precentral gyrus. He spoke aloud with the greatest difficulty, about three times more slowly than a normal subject. His inner speech was slowed in the same proportion. The non-verbal recognition time (gnosia) and that of the beginning of naming were within about normal limits.[17g, j]

In the case of a 65 year old woman with intact intelligence, suffering from progressive bulbar palsy with fasciculation of the muscles and slight signs of spasticity of the facial and trigeminal motor nerves, evoking a high form of *amyotrophic lateral sclerosis* (a motor neurone disease), speaking aloud was very difficult and took about twice as long as in a normal subject. The same was true of her inner speech.[17q]

It was with patients suffering from *Parkinson's disease* that I began my research on inner speech. In 1957 I demonstrated that, in a series of fifteen such patients, in each case inner and outer speech were slowed at the same rate, on an average of one half that of normal subjects. In my opinion this is one of the classic components of "bradypsychism," or the slowing of the mind, in Parkinson's disease.[17a] With Professor A. Werner, I had the opportunity of observing patients suffering from Parkinsonism before, during, and after stereotaxic operations on the *ventrolateral nucleus of the thalamus* (VOP). Each time I noticed a correlation between the speeds of both inner and outer speech, either slowing or accelerating.[17h]

The only possible explanation for these facts is that these neuro-motor structures, situated *below* the classical cerebral areas of language, similarly intervene in inner and outer speech. If we imagine that the classical cerebral structures of spoken language is a reservoir containing water under a certain pressure, everything happens as if the flow-pipe were constricted at different levels, the same holding for both inner and outer speech.

We could still object that, rigorously speaking, these observations do not prove that during inner speech the neuro-motor activities extend beyond the furthest peripheral examined level, i.e., the bulbar motor neurone. But the following could be said against such an objection: Firstly, we have no physiological reasons for thinking that the nerve message can stop half-way. Secondly, many records of muscular potentials were made during inner speech, particularly by Jacobson,[5, 6, 7, 8, 9] Faaborg-Anderson,[24] Edfeldt,[24, 25] and McGuigan.[10, 11, 12] Thirdly, we ourselves, with the help of a simple larygoscopic mirror, noticed movements of the vocal cords during inner speech in a large proportion of subjects and tests.[17c] Fourthly, inner speech is suppressed by deep relaxation of the speech muscles.[6] Here, in my opinion, we have a whole series of complementary research whose results converge.

I have had the opportunity to examine some patients after *laryngectomy*. It is not surprising that there was little or no modification of inner speech among these patients, and this is not in contradiction to the previous observations: in fact, in these patients the articulation muscles remain intact. On the other hand, the only patient with a laryngectomy whom we asked to evoke mentally a continuous note on a certain pitch was unable to do so.[17a] My friend Dr. Pommez, secretary of the *Société Française de Médecine de la Voix et de la Parole,* attaché at the Bordeaux Academy of Music, told me of similar observations.

Finally, in studying the times a stammerer takes to formulate the same sentence out loud and inwardly, "in thought," as well as the variation of these times with the same subject during the same test, we notice that if *stammering* is perhaps not totally absent from inner speech it is much more pronounced during outer speech. This undoubtedly means that the intensity of muscular tension aggravates the problem in the second case. It is also worth recalling that it is possible to lessen or to stop stammering simply by modifying the rhythm of speech or the intensity, pitch, or tone of the voice.[17p]

Now let us look at the question of possible motor components in visual imagination, or at least in certain forms of it.

We use simple outlines, sufficiently long and easy to recall, such as a zigzag line or the outline of three sail-boats, shown within a sufficiently wide angle. The subject must follow the contour visually as completely and quickly as possible, first looking at the object, then mentally, by memory, with his eyes closed. A hand signal marks the beginning and end of each test. Both outer and inner performances are slower in patients suffering from *Parkinson's syndrome,* and improve in the same proportion (after a temporary slowdown) after *thermocoagulation of the VOP.*[17h] The slowest subject before the operation was the most accelerated after.

The conclusions are the same as those having to do with the inner speech of these patients: certain forms of visual imagination require neuro-motor activities. Once again we confirm by another method the results of Jacobson,[5, 6, 7, 8, 9] McGuigan,[10, 11, 12] Morel,[26] Schifferli[27] and many others by electromyographical or direct, optical observation, to which we might add the suppression of visual imagery through the relaxation of the eye muscles.[6]

Some consequences of the motor-kinesthetic theory of certain forms of inner speech and visual imagination. Kinesthetic biofeedback. The two successive cerebral moments of spoken language.

One tends to see the classical, or nearly classical, cerebral structures of spoken language in the spatial form of a *trihedron* whose triangular cortical base would be delineated by the Wernicke, Broca, and Penfield areas, and whose apex would be neothalamic ("pyramid of language"). Confirming these views of Penfield[28] and other authors, I have had the opportunity to observe, with Professor Werner, transitory symptoms of aphasia (particularly of amnestic aphasia) during electrical stimulation near the left neothalamus in a stereotaxic procedure.[17r]

Whatever the exact extension of the central structures of spoken language may be, there are strong reasons to suppose that, during the first activity of these structures (following, for instance, that of areas related to the non-verbal recognition of the object), *the word appears before any verbal consciousness properly speaking, although the subject knows perfectly well (but in a non-verbal way) what he is about to say.* It is certain that the *outer* spoken word is followed by both auditory and kinesthetic retroactive afferences which allow the subject to hear and to feel what he said a fraction of a second before. It is no less certain that (except in the case of special interior preparation of speech, or in that of pathological "echo reading," whose study would be very interesting from these perspectives) one never has the impression of speaking twice successively when talking! In our opinion, verbal consciousness properly speaking appears only during this second cerebral activity corresponding to the integration of these retroactive afferences. The interval of time between these two successive moments may be some hundreds of milliseconds. If in the second moment one artificially introduces a time lapse between the arrivals of the auditory and the kinesthetic retroactive messages respectively (delayed speech feedback), major disturbances are observed in outer speech. In the case of total deafness, and also during inner speech (if its motor theory is correct), kinesthetic feedback alone intervenes, though less intensely in the second case. In the case where motor nerve activity does not reach the muscles in inner speech, shorter feedback circuits may be presumed. But, as we indicated above, this hypothesis is neurophysiologically improbable.[30, 17b, d, e, q, r, t, w]

The following seems to be a reasonable consequent: in the central structures of spoken language there probably exist some areas related to the kinesthetic integration of words, which work together with areas of auditory integration during the outer speech of normal subjects, and alone for the deaf and for normal subjects during the inner speech, though less intensely in the latter case.

We can also foresee the possibility of dissociated aphasia affecting only inner speech in the case of an isolated disorder of these kinesthetic areas of the brain, and that such a disturbance *("dysoro-verbo-kinesthesis")* could be observed by the study of whispered speech during a temporary, artificial suppression of auditory control by a deafening noise. In fact, with I. Spitzer, we have had the opportunity to observe such disturbances,[17u] and that may constitute a further argument in favor of the motor-kinesthetic theory of inner speech.[17q]

Analogous considerations apply in the visual tracking of an outline through a sufficiently wide angle, first by sight and then by memory. The experience, as I said, shows that the two visual activities also have a motor component.

Can the motor-kinesthetic theory be extended to hearing, to interior verbal processes with an auditive character, to fixed vision using both macular and peripheral fields, and to corresponding mental representations?

Contrary to Bergson's first opinion,[1] which he later recognized to be too absolute, and to the more recent views of Libermann ("motor theory of speech perception"[31]), the hearing and understanding of someone else's words would not require motor participation. Patients suffering from pure motor aphasia, or from an oro-verbal slowdown caused by a peripheral, neuro-motor disorder, hear and understand without the least difficulty or delay.

There are reasons to hold that the same would apply to the normal or pathological auditory or auditory-verbal persistence, when the noise, sounds, or words still "remain in our heads," as the saying goes, after something has just been heard.[17x] In fact, the experiments of Konorski confirm that in such a case nerve impulses do not extend beyond sensory structures. After a sufficiently long time, when we voluntarily remember words previously heard, the motor-proprioceptive component appears and increases, while the true auditory characteristics decrease. The particularities easiest to remember are possibly those which are most easily imitated in an interior, motor way: the rhythm of speech, the intensity, pitch, and certain details of the tone of the voice. It would be useful to ask musicians about the subject.

With the so called auditory-verbal automatisms, the question becomes more complicated in its relation to Jackson's theory.[17y] Penfield sets off "experiential responses" having both auditory and verbal characteristics by electrical stimulation at the level of the temporal cortex of both hemispheres, but more frequently of the left, major one.[28, 29] I personally observed stereotyped auditory-verbal automatisms during epileptic attacks in a right-handed patient with a pathological electroencephalographical focus on the right side of the brain.[17o] Maury's famous dream, which would have taken place entirely in the short space of time between the collapse of the bed canopy and the awakening of the dreamer, included long speeches attributed by the dreamer to himself and others, and ended by his being beheaded... All of this in no way favors the idea of a participation of the cerebral areas of spoken language located at the level of the dominant hemisphere, nor of the neuro-motor structures linked to them and which, with them, demand a certain *tempo*.[17m, s]

On the other hand certain patients suffering from auditory-verbal hallucinations, which they attribute to another, sometimes make little lip movements during their hallucinations, and it is possible to stop them temporarily by having the patients drink and glass of water, thus blocking their phonic and articulation muscles.[26] And I would add that, as our spouses can testify, many of us speak aloud while sleeping...

This difficult problem has given rise to much research, and here again I would like to refer to the work of Professor McGuigan.[10, 11, 12] Perhaps, as a provisional hypothesis, it may be admitted that automatic auditory-verbal processes include both motor and sensory structures. If Morel emphasized mouth movements during auditory-verbal hallucinations, he also noticed that during their hallucinations these patients showed diminished hearing.[26]

Do vision and visual imagination always require ocular movements? In my opinion all precise research on this subject must take into account both macular and peripheral vision and Wertheim's curves. These curves show a rapid lessening of visual acuity from the macula to the periphery of the visual field.

In our experiments designed to measure the times of non-verbal recognition and of naming, we were careful to display the objects within a small angle of vision and to ask the subject to fix his sight on a central phosphorescent point before the test was illuminated. However, even with these precautions we noticed a small difference in time between the start of naming, respectively, a color and a simple form (about 200 milliseconds longer for the latter), and this extra time could possibly include an ocular exploration which would not have been completely suppressed.[17j] On the other hand, in experiments designed to observe a correlative slowing of the visual tracking of a contour first seen and then represented mentally in patients suffering from peripheral neuro-motor disorders, we used objects presented in a large, open angle of vision and insisted on the necessity of precise vision: this, for the visual performance of the task, necessarily required macular vision and eye movement.

Indeed dreams, in which visual imagery dominates, are thought to take place during the so-called paradoxical phase of sleep, precisely where we observe eye movements. But it is also possible to observe such eye movements in new born babies, among the blind from birth, and in comas caused by functional suppression of the cerebral cortex. In addition, it is also during paradoxical sleep that the greatest relaxation of general musculature can be observed, contrasting with the eye movements; but during our dreams we not only have the impression of speaking aloud, of hearing, and above all of seeing, but also of moving. Is there or is there not a neuro-motor component in these dream images? And when a patient, after an amputation at the shoulder, has the illusion of moving his absent, imaginary fingers?[17m, s, v] And I myself, who underwent a complete removal of my right knee at the age of twenty-four, followed by the atrophy of my thigh muscles, and who thirty-three years later still dream of bending my knee without difficulty? During my didactic relaxation one night I dreamt of a kind of bodily disappearing, stopped by a sudden awakening. A few weeks earlier, after the first session, I dreamt that I was giving a splendid performance on a racing bicycle!

As with inner auditory-verbal patterns, perhaps we should consider visual imagination as moving along an axis with motor and sensory structures respectively at its two poles, sometimes closer to the one, sometimes to the other. Morel, for instance, observed that the visual hallucinations of patients suffering from *delirium tremens* correspond to an elliptic, positive macular scotoma vaguely evoking an animal and that, consequently, these patients imagine small animals to be near and large ones far away, both moving with the movements of the eyes.[26]

Some prospects.

The field of progressive relaxation and its associated methods is growing every day, and I am not qualified to describe it. To stick to my specialty, that of mental and nervous diseases, I shall just underline two facts. First of all, the huge proportion of patients showing signs of abnormal muscular tension and particularly of tetany in an average neuropsychiatric population: as I said earlier, 88% of my Geneva patients. Next, the fact that often tranquilizers relax muscles (e.g., diazepam) and neuroleptics slow them down (Parkinson's syndrome, e.g., butyrophenone). Are these secondary effects without a relationship to their effects on the mind? Or are the two kinds of effects linked together? Magnesium, which is itself so useful as a principal or supplementary medication in neuropsychiatry, has two kinds of actions: the relaxation of muscles and the diminution of general nervous overexcitability.[15]

I would not wish to conclude my talk without pointing out that certain spiritual technics, or simply psychological ones, undoubtedly have some relationship with progressive relaxation, which help us to master thought and emotions by bodily means: the old yoga technic of oriental mystics for dissipating illusory differences and losing themselves in the undifferentiated Unity;[32] the various "nights" of occidental mystics seeking a closeness to God, perhaps in a slightly more personal way; the unattached attention of the psychoanalyst in his concern with keeping an emotional neutrality while overcoming counter-transference, understanding his patient, and helping him to understand himself. Professor Wolpe, my friend Professor de Ajuriaguerra and other authors have mixed relaxation and psychotherapy in other, no less interesting ways.[33, 35]

Concerning the increasing number of those who are more concerned with immortality on earth, a few years ago I ventured to submit to them a problem more of the mechanical order: if, imagining possible or impossible futures in the tradition of Wells, we would perceive some of our distant descendants reduced—or dilated, sublimated, "quintessentiated"—to the state of simple irrigated brains connected to the outside by afferent and efferent electric signals, do we or do we not need to provide them with biofeedback for the retroactive auto-control of their activity?[17v] "The brain and the mind constitute a unity," wrote Lord Brain.[34] It is preferable to consider, with Professor Jacobson, that the body and the mind constitute a unity, part and parcel of the whole of reality: psychophysiology, environmental psychophysiology, and not neuropsychology.

Whatever the existence and extension of mental processes may be without actual neuromuscular concomitants, it still remains true that thought seems to be fundamentally an internalized action. Simply put, the internalization of movement would be more or less complete. Certain mental processes would still contain minuscule, covert movements, others would not. But there is no doubt that the latter also would have been formed, both phylogenetically and ontogenetically, in the course of the evolution of species and that of individuals, through the march and the rush towards life. For the struggle for life, at least among animals (who do not possess chlorophyll), requires movement: searching for pastures, tracking prey, fleeing predators. Such is probably one of the humble roots of the human mind.[18]

BIBLIOGRAPHY

1. H. Bergson: *Time and Free Will: An Essay on the Immediate Data of Consciousness.* Humanities Press, New York, 1971.

2. J. Piaget: *The Psychology of the Child.* Translated from the French by Helen Weaver, Basic Books, New York, 1969.

3. J. Piaget: *Mental Imagery in the Child.* Basic Books, New York, 1971.

4. I. Pavlov: *Selected Works.* Foreign Languages Publishing House, Moscow, 1955.

5. E. Jacobson: Electrophysiology of Mental Activities, Amer. J. Psychol., *44*, 1932, 677–694. Electrical Measurements of Mental Activities in Man, Trans. NY Acad. Sci., *8*, 1946, 272–273.

6. E. Jacobson: *Progressive Relaxation.* University of Chicago Press, Chicago, 1929; Midway Reprint, 1974.

7. E. Jacobson: *Tension in Medicine.* C. Thomas, Springfield, 1967.

8. E. Jacobson: *Biology of Emotions.* C. Thomas, Springfield, 1967.

9. E. Jacobson: *The Human Mind.* C. Thomas, Springfield, 1982.

10. F. J. McGuigan: *Thinking. Studies of Covert Language Behavior.* Appleton-Century-Crofts, New York, 1973.

11. F. J. McGuigan: *The Psychophysiology of Thinking. Studies of Covert Processes.* Academic Press, New York, 1973.

12. F. J. McGuigan: *Principles of Covert Behavior. A Study in Psychophysiology of Thinking.* Englewood Cliffs, N.J., Prentice Hall, 1978.

13. A. N. Sokolov: *Inner Speech and Thought.* Translated from Russian to English by T. Onischenko, Plenum Press, New York, London, 1972.

14. *11th World Congress of Neurology,* Excerpta Medica, International Congress Series no. 427, Amsterdam, Oxford, 1977.

15. Y. Chesni: "Intérêt du magnésium en neuropsychiatrie: Spasmophilie, autres affections, cas mixtes. Petite orientation statistique sur 50 malades choisis au hasard," Rev. Neurol., *132*, 12, 1976, 873.

16. Y. Chesni: *Dialectical Realism. Towards a Philosophy of Growth.* Translated from the French by J. P. Zenk, The Live Oak Press, Palo Alto, 1987.

17. Y. Chesni: Research on inner speech and visual imagination published under various titles in the following reviews: a Rev. Laryngol., *79*, 12, 1958, 1410–1444, Portmann, Bordeaux. b Rev. Laryngol. *81*, 3–4, 1960, 255–259. c Rev. Neurol., *102*, 6, 1960, 706–710. d Actes du 1er Congrès de Médecine Cybernétique, 316–320, S.M.C., Naples, 1962. e Rev. Laryngol., *84*, 7–8, 1963, 451–457. f Confinia Neurol., *23*, 1963, 189–196. g Archives Suisses Neurol., Neurochir., Psychiat., *91*, 2, 1963, 577. h Arch. Suisses Neurol., Neurochir., Psychiat., *94*, 2 1964, 249–264. i Confin. Neurol., *25*, 1965, 105–124. j Rev. Laryngol., *85*, 7–8, 1964, 581–593. k Arch. Suisses Neurol., Neurochir., Psychiat., *96*, 2, 1965, 366–378. l Confin. Neurol., *25*, 1965, 283–290. m Confin. Neurol., *28*, 3–4, 1966, 309–320, and 6, 1966 (rectification). n Rev. Laryngol., *87*, 3–4, 1966, 235–244. o Rev. Neurol., *115*, 5, 1966, 966–971. p Rev. Larygnol., *88*, 3–4, 1967, 219–226. q Act. Neurol. Psychiat. Belg., *67*, 11, 1967, 895–910. r Rev. Neurol., *116*, 6, 1967, 682–683. s Rev. Oto-Neuro-Opthalm., *XL*, 7,

1968, 361–366. t Cahiers d'Etudes Biologiques, 16–17, 1968, 9–29, Lethielleux, Paris. u Rev. Oto-Neuro-Opthalm., *XLI*, 5, 1969, 260–269. v Confin. Neurol., *31*, 1969, 374–382, and *32*, 1970, 384 (rectification). w Rev. Laryngol., *92*, 9–10, 1971, 541–545. x Rev. Laryngol., *92*, 3–4, 1971, 159–160. y Rev. Oto-Neuro-Ophtalm., *XLII*, 7, 1970, 416–422.

18. Y. Chesni: "Reflections concerning consciousness," in the present work.

19. J. C. Lilly, R. B. Cherry: Surface Movements of Click Responses from Acoustic Cortex of Cat. Leading and Trailing Edges of a Response Figure, J. Neurophysiol., *17*, 1954, 521–532.

20. E. Weigl: The Phenomenon of Temporary Deblocking in Aphasia, Z. f. Phon. Spr. u. Komm., 14, 1961, 337–364.

21. E. Weigl: Neuropsychology and Linguistics. Topics of Common Research, Foundations of Language, 6, 1970, 1–18.

22. A. Kreindler: *Performances in Aphasia. A Neurodynamical Diagnostic and Psychological Study.* Gauthier-Villars, Paris, 1968.

23. J. Emile: *Contribution à l'étude des paralysies pseudobulbaires corticales. Diplégie facio-linguo- masticatrice.* A.G.E.M.P., Paris, 1965.

24. F. Faaborg-Andersen, A. W. Edfeldt: Electromyography of Intrinsic and Extrinsic Laryngeal Muscles during Silent Speech. Correlation with Reading Activity, Act. Oto-Laryngol., *49*, 6, 1958, 478–482.

25. A. W. Edfeldt: *Silent Speech and Silent Reading.* Acta Universitatis Stockholmiensis, Stockholm Studies in Educational Psychology, 4, Almqvist & Wiksell, Stockholm, 1959.

26. F. Morel: *Introduction à la psychiatrie neurologique.* Masson, Paris, F. Roth, Lausanne, 1947.

27. P. Schifferli: *L'enregistrement photographique de la motricité oculaire dans l'exploration, dans la reconnaissance et dans la représentation visuelles.* Thèse de la Faculté de Médecine de Genève, 1953.

28. W. Penfield: *Speech and Brain Mechanisms.* Princeton University Press, Princeton, 1959.

29. W. Penfield, P. Perot: The Brain's Record of Auditory and Visual Experience, Brain, 86, 1963, 595–696.

30. V. M. Buscaino: Udito e linguaggio dal punto di vista neurobiologico. Attivita neuro-musculari e conseguenze propriocettive, Act. Neurol. Napoli, 15, 1962, 637–652.

31. A. M. Liberman: A Motor Theory of Speech Perception, Proceedings of the Speech Communication Seminar, *2*, Royal Institute of Technology, Stockholm, 1962.

32. M. Eliade: *Yoga: Immortality and Liberty.* Translated by R. Willard Trask, Princeton University Press, Princeton, 1970.

33. Colloquy on relaxation at the Clinique Psychiatrique Universitaire de Genève. Médecine et Hygiène, Geneva, 1975.

34. Lord Brain: *Clinical Neurology.* Oxford University Press, London, 1964.

35. J. Wolpe: *The Practice of Behavior Therapy.* Pergamon, Elmsford, 1982.